first time
CAKE DECORATING

Brimming with creative inspiration, how-to projects, and useful information to enrich your everyday life, Quarto Knows is a favorite destination for those pursuing their interests and passions. Visit our site and dig deeper with our books into your area of interest: Quarto Creates, Quarto Cooks, Quarto Homes, Quarto Lives, Quarto Drives, Quarto Explores, Quarto Gifts, or Quarto Kids.

© 2018 Quarto Publishing Group USA Inc.
Text © 2012 Quarto Publishing Group USA Inc.

First published in 2018 by Creative Publishing international, an imprint of The Quarto Group, 401 Second Avenue North, Suite 310, Minneapolis, MN 55401, USA.
T (612) 344-8100 F (612) 344-8692 QuartoKnows.com

Creative Publishing international titles are also available at discount for retail, wholesale, promotional, and bulk purchase. For details, contact the Special Sales Manager by email at specialsales@quarto.com or by mail at The Quarto Group, Attn: Special Sales Manager, 401 Second Avenue North, Suite 310, Minneapolis, MN 55401, USA.

10 9 8 7 6 5 4 3 2

ISBN: 978-1-58923-961-6

Digital edition published in 2018
eISBN: 978-1-63159-479-3

The content for this book previously appeared in *The Complete Photo Guide to Cake Decorating* (CPi, 2012) by Autumn Carpenter.

Originally found under the following Library of Congress Cataloging-in-Publication Data
Carpenter, Autumn.
The complete photo guide to cake decorating / Autumn Carpenter.
p. cm.
Summary: ""Reference for cake decorating methods, including basic cake preparation and materials, piping techniques, fondant and gum paste accents, and miscellaneous techniques"--Provided by publisher"-- Provided by publisher.
ISBN-13: 978-1-58923-669-1 (pbk.)
ISBN-10: 1-58923-669-6 (soft cover)
1. Cake decorating. 2. Cake decorating--Pictorial works. I. Title.
TX771.2.C37 2012
    641.86'53900222--dc23
2011028089

Design and Page Layout: Megan Jones Design
Photography: Dan Brand

Printed in China

first time

CAKE DECORATING

THE ABSOLUTE BEGINNER'S GUIDE

by Autumn Carpenter

Creative Publishing
international

contents

introduction

Celebrating special events with cake is tradition. Whether the party is a simple family affair or a full-blown extravaganza, the cake is an important part of the party. There is nothing like being a part of the party by sharing your talents. If you are a beginning decorator, this book will serve as a step-by-step course in cake decorating. If you are an experienced or professional decorator, this book will quickly become your go-to guide when seeking out new techniques.

The book is organized into four sections: basic cake preparation, piping techniques, fondant and gum paste accents, and miscellaneous techniques. Within the four sections there are chapters covering dozens of decorating techniques. Each technique is explained in steps and enhanced with full-color photographs. Tricks of the trade and troubleshooting tips are provided throughout to ensure you'll produce fabulously decorated cakes with ease.

The first section covers basic cake preparation. It is important to learn or review the basics before moving on to more detailed decorating. Baking basics, icing recipes, icing a cake, covering a cake with fondant, and cake charts are just a few of the basics covered in this section. The second section includes piping techniques for traditional, American-style decorating. Explore various decorating tips to create textures with icing. Rolled fondant and gum paste accents are covered in the third section. This edible claylike material provides a canvas for amazing decorating techniques. The final section covers miscellaneous techniques to further your decorating knowledge. Introductions to using advanced techniques and tools are covered.

Decorating has brought me so much joy; from fond memories of working with my mom on several projects, to the priceless joyous expressions on the guests of honor receiving the cakes. Now as co-owner of a confectionary supply store, Country Kitchen SweetArt, I am able to share my passion by teaching classes and assisting customers.

It is likely that cake decorating will soon become your passion. With practice and patience, you can become a great cake decorator. Have fun learning and remember: There is no right or wrong way to decorate a cake. Over time, you will develop a unique style. Cake decorating is an art and the iced cake is your canvas.

BASIC CAKE PREPARATION

It is important to start with a well-baked and smoothly iced cake before decorating. This section covers baking basics, icing recipes, and techniques. General instructions and several tips are included to ensure success for covering cakes in fondant or icing cakes with buttercream. This section also covers filling cakes, using food color, storing and transporting cakes, and additional beginning fundamentals.

tools for baking and decorating cakes

Below is a list of equipment needed to get started. Not all items are necessary, but the tools listed are practical and will make the baking, icing, and decorating process more enjoyable.

BRUSHES

Keep a variety of widths and styles of brushes on hand. These brushes should be used exclusively for cake decorating to avoid picking up odors and residue from other foods. Pastry brushes (1) may be used for greasing pans and to remove excess crumbs from a cake's surface before icing. Brushes with small, fine bristles (2) are used for painting details onto cakes and for adding edible glue to pieces when hand-molding. Flat brushes with squared edges (3) are ideal for brush embroidery and for applying color to gum paste flowers with dusting powder. Brushes with round, soft bristles (4) are used for applying dust over large surfaces. Use stencil brushes (5) for applying color on a cake with a stencil. Brushes may also be used to clean excess corn starch or powdered sugar from projects.

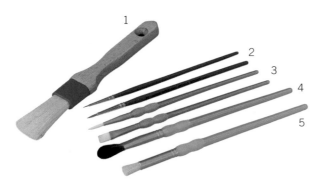

CAKE PANS

Dozens of shapes and sizes of cake pans can be found in cake and candy supply stores. Traditional shapes such as round, square, and rectangular (sheet cake) are versatile, come in several sizes, and are practical for many uses. Rectangular and square pans are available with sharp corners, which make a very attractive cake with crisp edges, or rounded corners, which make clean-up a breeze but the edges are not as professional-looking.

There are no industry standards on the size of a sheet cake pan. Traditionally, a 9" × 13" (23 × 33 cm) pan is a quarter sheet cake pan, a 12" × 18" (30.5 × 46 cm) pan is a half sheet cake pan and a 16" × 24" (4.5 × 61 cm) pan is a full sheet cake pan. Measure the inside of the oven before purchasing any large pans. There should be 1" (2.5 cm) space around the pan when placed in the oven so that air can properly circulate. For example, a full sheet cake pan, 16" × 24" (40.5 × 61 cm) will not fit in a standard oven.

Novelty pans are available in several themes and popular licensed characters. Be sure to thoroughly grease every crevice of these pans, as cake tends to stick to the details.

The typical height of cake pans is 2" (5 cm). Popular sizes of cake pans also are available in 3" (7.5 cm) height, but are more difficult to find.

Aluminum cake pans are what most bakers prefer. Heavy aluminum pans will withstand rough usage and are less likely to warp than lightweight aluminum. Cake pans with a dark finish tend to brown cakes quicker. Lower the oven temperature 25°F (20°C) if using dark pans. Stainless steel is not a good conductor of heat and is not the best type of bakeware for cakes.

Pantastic cake pans are a type of pan made of a plastic that can withstand temperatures up to 375°F (190°C). Pantastic cake pans are an affordable option to bake fun-shaped cakes and can be used several times. A cookie sheet should be placed under the Pantastic cake pan during baking. It is very important to grease and flour every area thoroughly.

Cake pans that are larger than 12" (30.5 cm) in diameter may require a heating core, which is put in the center of the cake pan during baking to ensure that the cake bakes evenly. Place a greased and floured core in the center of the grease and floured cake pan. Fill the cake pan and the heating core with cake batter. After baking, remove the core and release the core piece, leaving a hole in the cake. Fill the hole in the cake with the removed baked core piece.

CAKE SLICERS

Cake slicers are used to level the cake if it has a dome and to divide a cake layer for torting. A slicer with an adjustable blade allows the user more possibilities.

CAKE STRIPS AND CAKE TESTER

A cake tester (1) is a tool with a long stainless steel blade that is inserted into the cake to test for doneness. A toothpick may also be used. Insulated strips (2) are designed to keep the sides of the pan from becoming too hot, causing the cake to stop rising on the sides. These strips produce cakes with less of a dome and fewer cracks. To use, saturate the strips with water, squeeze out the excess, place around the outside of the cake pan, and secure with a straight pin.

COOLING RACKS

It is important for cakes to rest on a cooling rack after baking to insure even circulation.

SPONGES, PADS, AND FOAM SHEETS

Foam sheets and pads are used for cupping flowers and adding veins to flowers and leaves. Many double-sided foam pads are used with nonstick plastic rolling pins to manipulate fondant and gum paste shapes. One side of the foam is soft, while the other side is firm. Use the soft side for softening the edges of flower petals and for frilling (page 86). The firm side may be used for rolling and cutting. Some pads have holes for drying and shaping flowers.

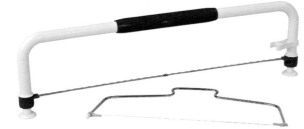

CLAY GUN/EXTRUDER

These extruders, developed for clay crafting, are great for making gum paste or rolled fondant lines and ropes with consistent thickness. Kits include a variety of interchangeable disks for making strands in different sizes and shapes.

CUTTERS FOR GUM PASTE AND FONDANT

Hundreds of cutters are available to efficiently cut gum paste strips, easily create flowers, make 3-D accents, and more! Cookie cutters can also be used. Letter cutters make professional-looking writing on cakes easy. Patchwork cutters can be used for a collage design or to emboss a design on the cake. Many plunger cutters will emboss details onto the cut gum paste. Materials for gum paste and fondant cutters vary from tin, stainless steel, to plastic. Care must be taken when washing, as tin may rust. Tin and stainless steel may bend when pressing the cutter, but give a sharp cut. Plastic may not give as sharp a cut, but is a good alternative to costly stainless steel cutters.

CUTTING TOOLS

A CelBoard is a perfectly smooth and flat surface to place small pieces of fondant or gum paste for cutting. A CelFlap is a clear sheet that is placed on top of rolled gum paste or fondant to keep pieces from drying.

The mini pizza cutter is handy for trimming excess fondant after covering the cake and for cutting strips and pieces of fondant or gum paste. Use a stainless steel ruler to ensure cut strips are straight. Thin flexible stainless steel blades can make micro-thin cuts without crushing the rolled fondant or gum paste. A pair of small scissors is used for snipping precise cuts in gum paste and fondant. A paring knife has many uses when decorating cakes. A bench scraper cuts easily through large chunks of fondant and gum paste. It is also handy for cleanup to scrape the work surface to remove crusted pieces of gum paste or fondant.

FONDANT SMOOTHERS

A fondant smoother gives a fondant-covered cake a satiny, smooth finish. Glide over the fondant-covered cake with one smoother while you hold the cake in place with the other to take out any wrinkles and give an even finish. Smoothing the cake with hands may leave unsightly indentations.

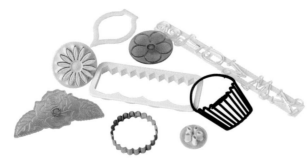

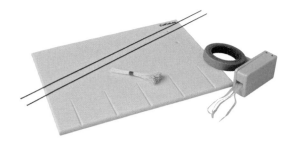

FLOUR SHAKER AND DUSTING POUCHES

A flour shaker or dusting pouch is used to prepare the work surface with cornstarch, powdered sugar, or a combination of the two when rolling fondant. Choose a shaker with fine mesh to ensure the work surface is not overdusted. Too much cornstarch or powdered sugar may dry out the rolled fondant. The dusting pouch gives just a slight dusting, which is ideal.

PARCHMENT PAPER AND CELLOPHANE WRAP

Sheets of parchment can be cut to fit cake pans before baking to ensure the cake will not stick. The pan should still be greased and floured. Parchment paper is also available in precut triangles to make disposable pastry bags (page 14). FDA-approved clear cellophane provides a wonderful surface for piping over patterns, which then easily peel off.

FLOWER FORMERS

To create flowers and accents with shape, place flat cut flowers in a flower former, gently press them to conform to the shape of the former, and allow them to dry.

FLOWER-MAKING TOOLS

Several thicknesses of wires are needed in gum paste floral making. Small dainty flowers look best when formed on thin wire. Other flowers require a stronger, thicker wire. The smaller the number of the wire gauge, the stronger the wire. Floral tape is needed to wrap wires and to create floral arrangements. Use white wire and floral tape if the flowers will be all white. Use green floral wire and tape for a realistic flower and stem. Stamens are available in several varieties to create flower centers—they are not edible. The back side of a CelBoard can be used to easily add wires to flowers and leaves. Other useful tools include modeling tools, small scissors, tweezers, and a CelPad for thinning petals.

ICING SPATULAS AND PALETTE KNIVES

Icing spatulas have a long, thin flexible blade. They are available angled (offset), straight, and tapered. Each length can be used for different purposes. A long, straight blade is used for icing the cake. Angled spatulas are helpful for spreading fillings. Small, tapered blades are handy for mixing small amounts of icing. Use palette knives for lifting cut gum paste pieces.

JUMBO CAKE LIFTER/JUMBO COOKIE SPATULA

This thin-bladed spatula, usually 10" or 12" (25.5 or 30.5 cm) in diameter, is used to slide layers onto one another. It is also used to easily lift the cake while icing and decorating.

MODELING TOOLS

A set of modeling tools is essential for hand-modeling. A basic starter kit should include ball tools in a variety of sizes, a tool with a cone at the end, a veining tool, and a dog bone tool. Other practical tools include a quilting wheel, shell tool, and scribing needle. CelSticks have a rounded end and a tapered, pointed end. CelSticks are the best tools to use for frilling and adding ruffles. Long, wooden dowels are used to shape curly ribbons.

MOLDS

Molds are an efficient way to decorate. Silicone molds are flexible, highly detailed, and allow gum paste to be easily released. Elegant lace and strands of beads can be made from silicone molds. Inexpensive candy molds can be used in cake decorating and can be found in almost any theme. Other molds can be found in craft stores, but they may not be food grade.

PASTA MACHINE

A pasta machine is useful if you do a lot of decorating with rolled fondant and gum paste accents. Free-standing crank machines are available, or attachments exist for some mixers. Generally, flowers and accents on cakes should be rolled very thin, while cut-outs that will be free-standing should be rolled slightly thicker. An alternative is to roll gum paste or fondant between two perfection strips of the same thickness.

PASTRY BAGS

Reusable pastry bags are economical and are offered in several sizes. Manufacturers' reusable pastry bags vary in size, weight, and material. Choose a pastry bag that is thin, lightweight, and conforms to your hand. A 12" (30.5 cm) bag is a standard size for common use. The smaller the pastry bag, the easier it is to control. Disposable pastry bags are convenient for clean-up. Pipe two colors at once with a disposable pastry bag divided into two sections. Fill each side with a different color and place them into a bag the same size fitted with a cake decorating tip. Parchment triangles are used to make pastry bags that are lightweight, economical, and disposable. Set aside pastry bags exclusively for royal icing. Buttercream and other fat-based icings may cause royal icing to break down.

ROLLING PINS

Smooth crusted buttercream cakes with a small pastry roller. Use a large, heavy rolling pin with a smooth finish to roll fondant. Rolling pins specially designed for rolled fondant are the best. Wooden rolling pins may show wood details. Silicone rolling pins work well for pastry and cookie dough but pick up lint, so are not the best choice for rolled fondant.

TIPS (TUBES) AND COUPLERS

Pipe a variety of shapes, sizes, and designs with decorating tips. Tip Usage, page 44, covers the most popular tips. Tip cleaning brushes have a small cylindrical brush for scrubbing the inside of the tips. Flower nails are available in several styles and allow the petals to be piped efficiently and consistently with the turn of the nail. A round nail is standard for most simple flowers.

Cake decorating tips (tubes) can be dropped into each bag. Gently tug on the tip to secure. The bag may need to be cut for larger tips or if using a coupler. A coupler is used to interchange tips while using the same pastry bag. It also helps keep the icing from seeping. A coupler has two parts: a base and a screw. The tip goes in between.

TEXTURE TOOLS

Add an embossed design to projects with a variety of texture tools. Rolling pins or texture sheets add an all-over pattern. Cutters can be used to emboss shapes and patterns. Crimpers are small tweezerlike tools used to press a design into a freshly covered rolled fondant cake.

TURNTABLE

A turntable is a valuable aid when icing and decorating a cake. The sides of cakes are much easier to ice if the cake can turn. When using a decorating comb, a turntable allows the cake to glide effortlessly while combing a design.

SCALE

A few instructions in this book list the measurement in grams. Grams are more accurate than ounces. Most digital scales convert ounces to grams easily and are available in a variety of price ranges.

VEINING MOLDS

Add realism to flower petals and leaves with veining molds.

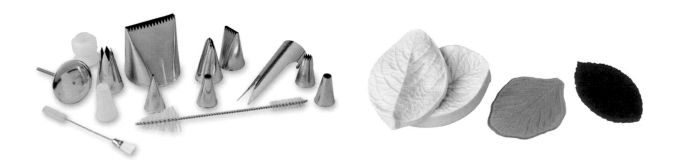

baking the cake

There are many cake recipe books or hundreds of recipes online, many of which are complete with ratings and baking suggestions, for baking a cake from scratch. For those who want to bake a cake quickly, commercial manufacturers of cake mixes have done a fantastic job perfecting their mix. Commercial cake mixes will vary in flavor, texture, and baking performance. Experiment with different brands to find the best flavor. If the cake does not taste fantastic, your work will not be fully appreciated.

BAKING INSTRUCTIONS

1 Brush on pan grease or grease and flour the inside of the pan. It is very important to thoroughly grease every crevice in shaped and novelty pans. Insulation strips (see page 11) can be used so that cakes will rise evenly. Dampen the strips with water, squeeze out the excess, and place the strips around the outside of the cake pan. Secure the strips with a straight pin.

2 Follow recipe instructions for mixing the cake batter. Fill the greased and flour-dusted pan with the cake batter approximately two-thirds full.

3 Bake according to the recipe instructions. Shortly before the time elapses, test if the cake is done by inserting a cake tester into the center of the cake. If the cake is done, the cake tester should come clean with just a few crumbs but no moist areas. The edges should begin to pull away and become golden. Place the baked cake on a cooling rack for 10 minutes. If the cake is too warm when removing it from the hot pan, the cake may crack or fall apart. Do not leave the

cake in the pan too long, or the cake will stick. The pan should be warm to the touch, but not hot or cooled completely.

4 If the cake did not rise evenly, or if the cake has a dome, level the top of the cake with a cake slicer or large bread knife. The cake may split when turned over if the top of the cake is not level.

5 When the cake pan is cool enough to handle, slide a knife along the edge of the pan.

6 Place a cooling rack on top of the pan. While holding the rack and pan securely together, flip the baked cake over with the cooling rack.

7 Slowly lift the cake pan straight up and away from the cake. Allow the cake to cool.

8 If the cake is still not level, use a cake slicer to even the top.

PAN GREASE

Pan Grease, or baker's grease, helps cakes release properly from pans. There is no need to flour the pan if Pan Grease is used. Simply brush a thick layer of Pan Grease onto the pan. Pan Grease is available in cake and candy supply stores. The pan may also be greased with a solid vegetable shortening and then dusted with flour.

A sheet of parchment paper can be cut to fit the pan to ensure the bottom of the cake will not stick. It is still important to grease and flour the cake pan even if using parchment.

FACTORS THAT WILL AFFECT HOW THE CAKE BAKES

Inaccurate Oven Temperature

An oven thermometer can be used to ensure the oven is baking at the proper temperature. Place an oven thermometer in the oven and compare the reading with the temperature set on the oven. If the reading is off, adjust the temperature accordingly.

Oven Placement

It is best to bake cakes in the middle of the oven on the center rack. If multiple cakes are on the center rack, allow 1" (2.5 cm) of space all around each pan. The cake pans should not touch each other or the sides of the oven. If a convection oven is used, the cakes will take less time to bake and should be baked at a lower temperature than the recipe dictates. Convection ovens circulate the air throughout the oven so that several cakes can be baked at once. However, overloading an oven with too many cakes may cause the cake batter to rise unevenly.

Mixing

Precisely follow the mixing instructions. Overmixed cake may not rise properly and may be dry. Undermixed cakes may also not rise properly and may have large air holes throughout the baked cake. Cake batter should be baked soon after it is mixed. This is more important for some batters than others. Cake batters with baking soda and baking powder need to be baked immediately after mixing. Letting batter sit for several minutes may cause the cake to be dense and flat.

Bake Time

If the cake is underbaked, it will fall in the center. If the cake is overbaked, it will be tough and dry. The oven door should not be opened during baking, as this may cause the cake to deflate.

TREATS

Make some tasty bite-sized cake treats with cake scraps and leftover icing. Crumble cake scraps in a bowl and stir in leftover icing. Add icing until the mixture is firm enough to roll. Roll into bite-sized bon-bons. Dip in melted chocolate and allow to set.

torting and filling cakes

Filling can be added in between cake layers, or add additional flavor and drama by torting the layers. Torting a cake can be done with a cake slicer or a serrated knife. A cake slicer is preferred as it will ensure that the cake layer is evenly cut.

To contain the filling, first pipe a dam around the edges using the same icing that will be used to ice the cake. If the cake will be covered in fondant, buttercream icing should be used for the dam. A dam is not necessary if the filling is the same as the outer icing. Allow about ¼" (6 mm) of space between the dam and the edge of the cake, so when the top layer is placed on the cake, pressure will push the icing on the dam, but not squirt out the sides of the cake.

1 Place the cake on an even surface. Adjust a cake slicer to the desired height. Insert the cake slicer into the side of the cake. Keeping the feet level with the surface, slide the cake slicer back and forth to cut into the cake. Do not lift the feet of the cake slicer while slicing. Lift the top layer of the cut cake using a jumbo cake lifter or a cookie sheet with no sides. Set top layer aside.

2 Fill a pastry bag with buttercream icing, or whatever icing will be used. With tip #1A, pipe a dam of icing around the edge of the cake.

3 Fill a pastry bag with cake filling. Squirt filling in the center of the cake. Then, with an offset spatula, spread filling to the edges of the dam.

4 Align the top layer with the bottom layer, and slide the top layer back onto the cake.

filling recipes

Filling transforms a basic cake into a gourmet layered cake with additional flavor and moisture. Cake fillings should complement the cake's flavor but not overpower. Most often, a thin layer of filling is all that is needed. If the fillings are spread too thickly, the flavor may overwhelm. Cakes filled with perishable ingredients such as fresh fruit should be refrigerated until served.

COMMERCIAL PASTRY FILLINGS

Commercial pastry fillings are a delicious, quick, and easy way to add a filling in cakes. These fillings are available in a variety of fruit flavors and cream fillings. Cakes filled with most commercial pastry fillings do not need to be refrigerated.

fudge filling recipe

- 1⅓ cups (330 g) marshmallow crème
- 1½ cups (300 g) sugar
- ⅔ cup (160 mL) evaporated milk
- ¼ cup (56 g) butter
- ¼ teaspoon (1 g) salt
- 3 cups dark chocolate (semi-sweet) (480 g), melted
- ½ cup (120 mL) hot water
- 1 teaspoon (5 mL) vanilla extract

In a large heavy saucepan over medium heat, combine marshmallow crème, sugar, evaporated milk, butter, and salt. Stir constantly and vigorously while bringing to a full boil and cook for 5 minutes, stirring constantly. Remove from heat and allow to cool until lukewarm. Stir in melted chocolate until smooth. Add hot water and vanilla. Stir until smooth. Allow to cool before filling. Fudge mixture will be soft.

Yield: 3 cups (750 mL)

caramel filling recipe

- ½ cup (113 g) butter
- 1 cup (230 g) packed brown sugar
- ¼ teaspoon (1 g) salt
- 6 tablespoons (90 mL) milk
- 3 cups (345 g) powdered sugar

Melt butter. Stir in brown sugar and salt. Boil for 2 minutes, stirring constantly. Remove from heat, add milk, and return to heat. Bring to rolling boil. Cool to lukewarm and stir in powdered sugar. Allow to cool before filling.

Yield: 2½ cups (625 mL)

FRESH FRUIT FILLING

Cakes with cream fillings and fresh fruit are especially elegant. Typically a layer of light filling is spread on the cake followed with a layer of fresh fruit. Cakes with fresh fruit fillings should be assembled and decorated just a few hours before serving. They also require refrigeration until served. Juice from fresh fruit may seep through the icing, so it is very important the fruit is dry. Thoroughly wash and cut the fruit. Lay the fruit on paper towels to dry.

ICINGS USED AS A FILLING

Several types of icing make delicious fillings. Whipped icing is a light, mildly sweet icing that is delectable in cupcakes and cakes. Buttercream icing adds extra sweetness to the cake. Ganache adds a richness like no other filling. These icings can also be enhanced with the addition of flavorings or icing fruits. For example, transform a basic chocolate cake into a mocha truffle cake by using a ganache filling with coffee flavor and chocolate.

icing recipes

CREAM CHEESE ICING

Cream cheese icing has a delicate richness that makes it delicious on almost any cake. The cake can be decorated with simple, piped borders using this icing, but the icing is too soft for detailed piping.

Storing Cream Cheese Icing

Unused cream cheese icing can be kept in an airtight container in the refrigerator for two weeks. Cakes with cream cheese icing can be kept at room temperature for one or two days. Keeping the cake in the refrigerator will prolong the shelf life of the cake, but condensation may form on the icing, causing the icing to have a grainy texture.

cream cheese icing recipe

1 (8 ounce; 224 g) package cream cheese, softened

¼ cup (45.5 g) butter, softened

2 tablespoons (31 g) sour cream

2 teaspoons (10 mL) vanilla extract

5 cups (650 g) confectioners' sugar

Beat cream cheese, butter, sour cream, and vanilla in large bowl until light and fluffy. Gradually beat in confectioners' sugar until smooth.

Yield: 5 cups (1.2 L)

BUTTERCREAM

Buttercream is a sweet, fluffy icing that is a traditional American favorite. A cake can be iced and decorated in buttercream, which will crust on the outside but remain creamy on the inside. Thinned buttercream is used to give a cake a crumb coat. Flowers made with buttercream may require a stiffer icing. Add less water to obtain a firmer consistency. Buttercream icing is also available premade at cake and candy supply stores.

Storing Buttercream

Cakes that are iced and decorated with buttercream will most likely form a crust. Humidity may affect the icing's ability to crust. Iced and decorated cakes with buttercream can be kept at room temperature for three to four days. Extreme warm temperatures can cause the icing to soften and melt. Refrigerating iced and decorated cakes with buttercream may cause condensation, making colors bleed.

Chocolate Buttercream Icing

A delicious chocolate buttercream icing can be made with the simple addition of cocoa powder. Add approximately 1 cup (110 g) of cocoa powder to the buttercream recipe. The cocoa powder may cause the buttercream to stiffen. Add a small amount of water to achieve the desired consistency.

buttercream icing recipe

½ cup (120 mL) high ratio shortening

4 cups (520 g) powdered sugar, sifted

5 tablespoons (75 mL) water

½ teaspoon (2.5 mL) salt

1 teaspoon (5 mL) vanilla flavoring

½ teaspoon (2.5 mL) almond flavoring

¼ teaspoon (1.5 mL) butter flavoring

In a large bowl, combine ingredients; beat on low speed until well blended. Continue beating on low speed for 10 minutes or until very creamy. Keep the bowl covered to prevent the icing from drying out. Unused icing can be kept in the refrigerator up to six weeks. Rewhip on low speed.

Yield: 4 cups (1 L)

PERFECTING BUTTERCREAM

* For a bright white icing, use clear flavorings. Pure vanilla will give the icing an ivory hue.

* Solid vegetable shortening can be substituted for high ratio shortening, a baker's quality shortening used in icing and cake recipes. High ratio shortening gives the icing a fine, smooth, and creamy texture without a greasy aftertaste. Solid vegetable shortening may affect the icing consistency and texture.

* Do not whip the icing on medium or high speed after the ingredients are blended. Extra air will be incorporated, causing bubbles.

* Dark colors in buttercream icing may deepen upon setting. Allow the icing to set for two to three hours to see true color.

ROYAL ICING

Royal icing has a variety of uses in cake decorating. It dries very hard, so this is not an appropriate icing for covering a cake. Many projects made with royal icing can be made several days in advance. Flowers piped with royal icing will be lightweight and have crisp petals. Royal icing is used for details on fondant-covered cakes and in stencils (see page 120). It is commonly used as a "glue" to assemble gingerbread houses. Use either of the following two recipes. Or, if you prefer, commercial premade royal icing mixes are available for convenience. Simply add water to the powdered mix and beat on high for several minutes.

Storing Royal Icing

Royal icing dries and forms a crust quickly, so always keep the bowl covered with a damp towel. Royal icing made with egg whites should be used immediately. Royal icing made with meringue powder will keep up to two weeks. Keep the icing in an airtight container at room temperature. Re-whip on high speed before piping. Flowers and accents made with royal icing can be stored in an airtight container for several months. Keep the container away from light to avoid the color fading.

PERFECTING ROYAL ICING

* Sifting the powdered sugar is important for piping to keep tips from becoming clogged. Use a sifter with a very fine mesh screen.

* Royal icing will break down with the presence of grease. Be sure all utensils and bowls are completely grease-free. Piping royal icing on buttercream may cause grease spots to form.

royal icing recipe with meringue powder

- 4 tablespoons (50 g) meringue powder
- ½ teaspoon (2 g) cream of tartar
- ⅔ cup (160 mL) water
- 8 cups (1.4 kg) powdered sugar, sifted
- 1 tablespoon (12.5 g) gum arabic

In a mixing bowl, combine meringue powder, cream of tartar, and water. Beat on high speed until stiff peaks form. In a separate bowl, stir together powdered sugar and gum arabic. Mix thoroughly and add to meringue. Beat on low speed until ingredients are incorporated, then mix on high speed for several minutes until stiff peaks form. Keep icing covered with a damp towel.

Yield: 4¾ cups (1.175 L)

royal icing recipe with egg white

- 1 pound (450 g) powdered sugar
- 3 large egg whites at room temperature
- ⅛ teaspoon (1.5 g) cream of tartar

Sift powdered sugar. Pour the egg whites into a mixing bowl. Mix in the cream of tartar and powdered sugar. After all the ingredients are incorporated, beat on high speed until stiff peaks form. Keep icing covered with a damp towel.

Yield: 2½ cups (625 mL)

food color

Colors make a cake stand out. Obtaining the right color and shade is the tricky part. Most jars of color will have a picture of the color; however, many factors can cause the color to vary. To test, mix a small amount of color with a small amount of icing before adding color to the full batch of icing. Most food colorings do not have an expiration date; however, the color can separate, harden, or change over time. For best results, keep food coloring no longer than a year.

TYPES OF COLORS

Powdered Food Colors

Powdered food colors are highly concentrated. It is best to dissolve the powdered granules before mixing the coloring into the icing to avoid specks. For buttercream and rolled fondant, blend a small amount of vegetable shortening with the powdered food color.

Gel and Paste Food Colors

Gel food colors are water-based and are highly concentrated. Many brands come in convenient and mess-free squeeze tubes. Other brands come in small jars. Use a clean toothpick to remove color from the jar to avoid contamination of the jar. Most manufacturers have switched from paste to gel, which has a longer shelf life.

> **REVIVING PASTE**
>
> If a jar of paste food color has thickened, add a few drops of glycerin to help revive the paste.

Liquid Food Colors

Liquid food colors are commonly found at grocery stores and are best suited for pastel colors. They are not as concentrated as gels, pastes, and powders.

Airbrush Food Colors

Only liquid colors should be used in an airbrush. It can be used in almost any icing, but it is difficult to achieve dark shades.

Oil-Based Food Colors

Oil-based food colors are used in coloring ganache icing and for coloring candy coatings and chocolate.

Natural Food Colors

Ingredients such as beets, red cabbage, and other plant extracts may add a slight flavor to the icing and the hues may be less vibrant than artificial colors, especially if cooked at high temperatures.

Dusting Powders

Dusting powders are available in a matte, pearl, or shimmer finish. They are used to brush color onto finished decorated products such as gum paste flowers—not to mix with icing or fondant.

Luster dust comes in dozens of colors including metallics. Pearl dusts have a pearlized white finish. Super pearl dust will add a sheen to any color. Sparkle dusts have a coarser grain than luster or pearl dusts, so the sparkle is a little more brilliant. Ultra white sparkle is especially pretty on flowers for a shimmery, dewy effect. Dusting powders can be brushed on dry, or the powder can be mixed with grain alcohol.

Food Color Markers

Markers containing food color are a convenient method of applying color onto hard surfaces.

HELPFUL INFORMATION ON FOOD COLORS

Dark Colors

Dark colors such as red, burgundy, dark purple, dark blue, and black require a lot of food color. Too much coloring may make the icing bitter and may also stain the mouth. For best results, use food color gels or paste. Mix dark colors into buttercream at least an hour ahead of time so they can intensify. Add white icing if the color becomes too dark.

Brown Icing

Mix cocoa powder with vegetable shortening to make a dark paste. Blend the cocoa paste into rolled fondant or buttercream. If the cocoa powder thickens the buttercream, thin with a small amount of water.

Black Icing

The most difficult to achieve. Follow the instructions above for making icing brown, then add black food color.

Red Icing

Red icing is also difficult to achieve. Some reds appear orange-red; while others look dark pink. Super red is a highly concentrated vibrant red.

A lot of red food coloring may create a bitter flavor. A "no taste" red is available and may be used with another red or by itself.

Color Fading

Fading can be discouraging. Colors that are likely to fade are red, pink, lavender, purple, peach, black, and gray. There are food colors available that are no-fade. Keep the cake in a cool, dark room or in a covered box to reduce fading.

Colors Darkening

Buttercream often darkens after an hour or two. Mix the icing with the food color several hours before decorating to see how the colors intensify. Colors fade in most other icings such as rolled fondant and royal icing.

Color Bleeding

Colors may bleed when moisture affects the icing. For best results, allow the buttercream to crust completely before adding a contrasting color. Adding details to a frozen iced cake may cause colors to bleed. Allow the cake to come to room temperature before adding any details. Cakes served outdoors in hot weather may also have icing that bleeds. To avoid bleeding, it is important to store the cake properly. Placing a buttercream iced and decorated cake in the refrigerator will add moisture and colors may bleed. Keeping the cake in an airtight container will cause condensation, which may cause bleeding. To keep bleeding at a minimum, place cakes in a loosely covered cake box to allow the cake to breathe. If bleeding is a concern, wait until the last minute to pipe contrasting colors.

Acid Ingredients in the Icing

If the recipe contains lemon juice, or other ingredients with acid, the actual color may vary.

Food Color Controversy

Food colors are strictly studied, regulated, and monitored by the Food and Drug Administration. A common theory that originated in the 1970s was that some food color caused hyperactivity. Results were reviewed from the FDA and the European Food Safety Authority independently. Each concluded that the study does not substantiate a link between the color additives and behavioral effects. All food colors are subject to ongoing safety review from the FDA as scientific understanding and methods of testing continue to improve.

COLORING ICINGS

1 Before mixing color, ensure that all icing ingredients are thoroughly combined. Add a small amount of food color to the icing. Use a toothpick for color in jars, or if the color is in tubes, squeeze the color into the icing.

2 Blend until all color is thoroughly added. There should be no streaks of color. If the color is too dark, add white icing. If the color is too light, add a little more color.

COLORING ROLLED FONDANT

3 Start with kneaded and soft rolled fondant. Add color to the fondant by using a toothpick for color in jars, or squeeze the color onto the fondant if the color is in tubes.

4 Begin kneading the color into the fondant. Add more color if necessary, to darken.

5 Knead thoroughly until there are no streaks of color.

icing a cake in buttercream

Icing a cake requires practice. Placing the cake on a turntable allows the pressure to be consistent when icing the sides. It is difficult to spread icing onto the cake without crumbs mixing with the icing. These two methods of icing keep crumbs at a minimum.

QUICK ICER METHOD

1 Place the cake on a cardboard of the same size to keep the work surface tidy and free of crumbs. Ice the cardboard as though it is part of the cake. Use a pastry brush to remove excess crumbs from the cake before icing. Place the quick icer tip, tip #789, in a large pastry bag with one-quarter of the tip showing. Fill the bag two-thirds full with icing. Holding the bag at a 45° angle, touch the surface of the cake.

2 Pipe a band of icing around the bottom of the cake, gently pressing against the cake while piping. Pipe an additional row of icing above that band, overlapping the row underneath and always gently pressing against the surface of the cake to keep the icing from falling. If necessary, pipe additional rows of icing until you reach the top of the cake.

3 Pipe bands of icing on the top of the cake, overlapping each band until the cake is not visible.

4 Use a long spatula to spread the icing. Smooth the top of the cake with long strokes. Then hold the spatula perpendicular to the turntable when icing the sides. Use one of the smoothing techniques in this chapter to smooth the buttercream.

CRUMB COAT METHOD

1 Place the cake on a cardboard of the same size to keep the work surface tidy and free of crumbs. While icing, ice the cardboard as though it is part of the cake. Mix a small amount of icing with water to thin the buttercream. The amount of water needed will vary according to the consistency of the icing. In general, for an 8" (20 cm) cake, mix approximately 1 cup of icing with 1 teaspoon of water. Spread the thinned icing on the cake to form a crumb coat. Allow the crumb coat to form a crust (usually 20–45 minutes).

2 After the crumb coat has set, place a large amount of icing on the top of the cake.

3 With a long spatula, spread the icing on the top using long strokes and gliding toward the edge.

4 Apply icing to the side of the cake. Hold the spatula perpendicular to the turntable when spreading the icing on the sides. Blend the icing from the top with the icing on the sides.

Glide the spatula along the top and sides of the cake to smooth. Use one of the smoothing techniques on the next page to smooth the buttercream.

CRUMB CONTROL

When crumb coating, keep two bowls for the icing. One bowl should be filled with icing free of crumbs. Use the other bowl to scrape the spatula and remove excess icing with crumbs after icing.

SMOOTHING THE ICING

Use any or a combination of the following techniques to give the buttercream a smooth, silky coating. The hot spatula blade method is used during the icing process. The pastry roller and the paper towel method are used after the icing has formed a crust.

1 The icing can be smoothed by dipping a spatula in hot water and completely drying the blade. The hot metal blade will slightly melt the icing to give a smooth finish. Use the hot spatula before the icing forms a crust.

2 A pastry roller may also be used to smooth the icing. After the icing forms a crust (approximately 45 minutes), gently roll over any areas that are not smooth with a pastry roller.

3 A paper towel can be used to smooth. Choose a paper towel with minimal texture. Allow the buttercream icing to form a crust and gently press the paper towel onto the icing.

buttercream iced cakes with texture

A cake can be minimally decorated with textured icing. Timing is very important to be successful when applying texture to buttercream iced cakes.

CAKE COMBS

Cake combs are available at cake decorating supply stores in a variety of designs and give cakes decorative ridges. Cake combs should be used on the buttercream icing after the icing has been smoothed, but before it forms a crust.

1 Hold the cake comb perpendicular with the turntable. Apply gentle pressure after the icing has been smoothed. Turn the turntable with one hand while gliding the cake comb along the side with the other hand. Move the hand up and down to achieve a wave pattern, as shown.

TEXTURE SHEETS

Texture sheets are available in a variety of designs and materials. Timing is crucial when adding texture with a texture mat. If not enough time was permitted for the buttercream icing to form a crust, the icing will stick to the texture mat. If too much time was allowed, the icing will crack.

2 Ice the cake with buttercream. Allow the buttercream icing to crust (usually about 45 minutes). Place the texture mat on top of the cake. With firm pressure, roll over the texture mat with a pastry roller. Do not roll back and forth, or double lines will be produced. Lift mat.

3 To texture the sides, place the texture mat against the cake. Firmly press mat into the cake to emboss texture. Lift mat.

covering a cake with rolled fondant

Rolled fondant gives a smooth, clean iced finish that is incomparable to other icings. The cake should be covered with an icing before being covered with fondant. The undericing gives the fondant a smooth, clean surface and adds additional sweetness. The cake should also be placed on a cardboard the same size as the baked cake (not larger). This makes moving the cake while working easier and keeps the work surface clean and free of crumbs. The instructions are for a cake with buttercream icing underneath, but other icings may be used.

GENERAL COVERING OF CAKES

1 Place the cake on a same-size cardboard; ice with buttercream. Allow the buttercream to crust completely, then brush on a layer of piping gel so the fondant will adhere to the cake. Knead and soften fondant. Dust the work surface sparingly with cornstarch (too much will dry out the fondant). Flatten fondant to approximately 2" (5 cm) thick. This will make rolling easier with a large ball. Using a lot of pressure, roll over the flattened fondant 2 times, then lift and turn fondant a quarter turn. Make certain the fondant is not sticking to the surface; if it is, dust with additional cornstarch. Do not flip the fondant over.

2 Repeat rolling and turning quarter turns. Turning the fondant will ensure it maintains an even shape. Continue rolling until fondant is approximately ⅛" (3 mm) thick. Be sure enough fondant is rolled to cover the cake. For this 8" × 3" (20 × 7.5 cm) cake, fondant 15" (38 cm) diameter is needed. Lift the fondant by rolling the fondant onto a long rolling pin.

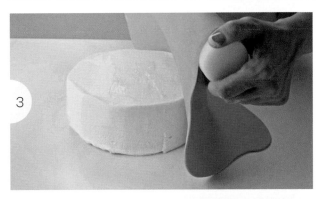

3 Unroll the fondant onto the cake.

4 Lift and shift the sides to eliminate any creases. Take care not to stretch and pull the fondant. Secure the edges by pressing palms against the sides of the cake.

5 With a mini pizza cutter, cut away excess fondant, leaving approximately 1" (2.5 cm).

6 Place cake on a bucket or bowl with a slightly smaller diameter. Rest one fondant smoother on top of the cake to hold it steady. Do not apply pressure or the smoother will impress lines. Smooth the sides with another smoother. Still holding the smoother on the top of the cake, hold a paring knife perpendicular to the cake and cut excess fondant.

7 Spread buttercream or other icing on cake board (see page 34). With a jumbo cake lifter or jumbo cookie spatula, transfer the fondant-covered cake to the cake board.

8 Use fondant smoothers to smooth the top and side of the cake.

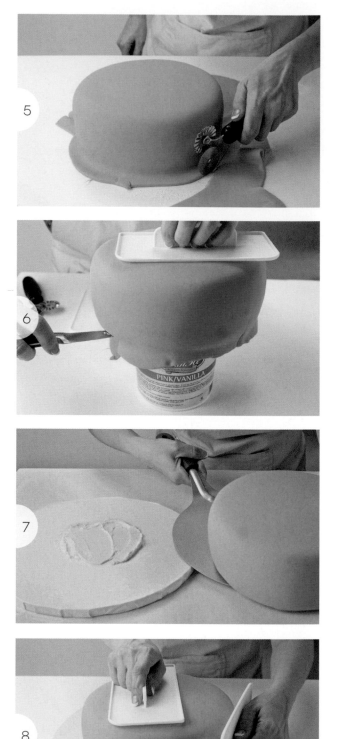

HOW MUCH FONDANT DO I NEED?

A circle of fondant should be the diameter of the cake plus the height of the cake doubled plus approximately 1" (2.5 cm) to allow for placement if the fondant is not perfectly centered. For example, an 8" (20 cm) cake that is 3" (7.5 cm) tall will need a 15" (38 cm) circle or square of fondant (8 + 3 + 3 + 1 = 15, or in centimeters: 20 + 7.5 + 7.5 + 3 = 38).

PERFECTING FONDANT

* The work surface should be completely clean. Do not wear clothing with a lot of lint or jewelry.

* Use cornstarch or a combination of cornstarch and powdered sugar to dust the countertop. Powdered sugar often dissolves into the rolled fondant, making it stick more than cornstarch.

* Use a straight pin to poke air bubbles then gently press with a clean, dry finger to release air. Use a fondant smoother to eliminate the hole.

* Work quickly. The fondant may develop tiny cracks or "elephant skin" if too much time elapses. Try to complete all the steps within seven minutes.

* Clammy hands, excess food color, and humidity can affect the consistency of the rolled fondant. If the fondant is sticky, knead in some powdered sugar. If the fondant is dry, knead in a small amount of solid vegetable shortening.

* Rolled fondant must be tightly wrapped in plastic wrap when not in use; otherwise, sections of the fondant will crust, become hard, and be unusable. If any fondant has crusted, cut that area off before kneading.

* When purchasing commercial rolled fondant, be sure it is for cake decorating. Dry fondant and candy fondant are used in candy-making.

storage and transportation of cakes

STORING CAKES

Icing and filling determine how a cake should be stored. Most cakes are fine left at room temperature. Keep decorated cakes away from sunlight to prevent fading. Heat may cause icings to melt. Protect the cake by placing it in a cake box or cardboard box until it is ready to be served. If the cake will not be eaten within 3 days, consider freezing it. Cakes with fresh cream fillings or fresh fruit must be refrigerated and eaten within a day or two.

FREEZING CAKES

The cake can be frozen without icing or may be completely iced. A cake that is not iced should be wrapped with plastic wrap before boxing. A cake that is decorated and iced with buttercream can be frozen in most cases. However, colors are likely to bleed when thawing. Consider adding the color after the cake is completely thawed. Rolled fondant does not freeze well, as condensation forms, causing tiny speckles. Place cake in box. Wrap cake tightly with three layers of plastic wrap, a layer of aluminum foil, and another layer of plastic wrap. Place in freezer. To defrost, place cake on counter and do not unwrap until it has completely come to room temperature. For the freshest tasting cakes, freeze no longer than one month.

TRANSPORTING CAKES

A cake should be placed in a box the same size as the cake base to prevent sliding. Place the box on a level surface. A sheet of foam rubber or a non-slip rug works well to prevent the box from sliding.

cake boards

The board or plate that the cake sits on should be attractive, but not detract from the cake. For example, if a cake is iced, decorated all in white, and sitting on a red foil-covered board, the eye will go directly to the bright board instead of the cake. There are a variety of materials and thicknesses of cake boards. The cake board must be sturdy enough to withstand the weight of the cake. For a simple iced and decorated cake, a board slightly bigger than the cake will suffice. Often, because of the aesthetics or design of the cake, there is no room for writing on the cake. The board can be used as an additional decorating surface. Design the cake first, then choose the proper size of board.

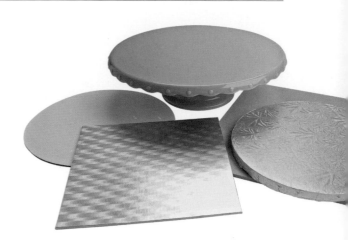

CAKE DRUMS

Cake drums are a thick, corrugated cardboard, usually ¼" to ½" (6 to 13 mm) thick and wrapped with decorative foil. These drums are sturdy enough to be used as a base for a birthday cake or tiered wedding cake.

CARDBOARDS

Precut cardboards in a variety of shapes and sizes are available for small, lightweight cakes. The cardboards should be wrapped with foil so that the moisture from the cake and icing does not warp or weaken the cardboard. Cardboards are available prewrapped with foil, or FDA-approved foils are available to cover the cardboards. Some cardboards are waxed and do not require wrapping with foil; however, they are not as attractive as the wrapped boards. Cardboards are also useful when decorating. In many cases it is nice to put a baked and cooled cake on a waxed cake cardboard the same size as the cake. When

icing the cake, the cardboard is iced as though it is part of the cake. This keeps the work area free of crumbs after the cake is iced. Slide a jumbo spatula or a cookie sheet with no sides under the cardboard to maneuver the cake.

MASONITE BOARDS

Masonite boards are much more durable than traditional cake cardboards or cake drums. Masonite boards are made of compressed fibers and will last for several uses. They are ideal to use for tiered cakes. These boards can be covered with decorative foil.

DECORATIVE BOARDS AND PLATES

Cakes placed on decorative cake stands and plates look exceptionally beautiful. Before icing or decorating the cake, place the cake on a waxed cardboard the same size as the cake. When icing the cake, the cardboard is iced as though it is part of the cake. Place a bit of icing on the decorative plate and set the iced cake on top. Add additional decorations and a border after it is on the plate. Lift the cardboard off the decorative plate before cutting and serving to protect the plate.

stacking cakes

Make a simple cake extra-special by adding tiers. It is important to stack cakes with support or the cake may fall.

This is a simple technique for the occasional stacked cake. Choose plastic plates or cake boards that are grease-resistant. The dowels used are ¾" (2 cm) diameter. Be sure the dowels are cut to the height of the icing. If there is extra height, there will be a gap in between tiers. The Smart Marker (optional) ensures the tiers are centered.

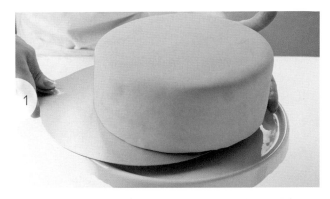

1 Spread some icing on a sturdy base plate. Place the bottom tier on the base plate. The remaining tiers should be placed on a grease-resistant plate of the same size.

2 Place the Smart Marker on the bottom tier. Line up the ring with the size of the cake. Find the ring that is the same size as the tier to be stacked and mark by pushing a toothpick or other pointed tool through the ring openings onto the larger cake.

3 Insert one dowel into the iced cake about ½" (1 cm) inside the dots marked, resting the dowel on the base board. Mark the height of the cake. Remove the dowel. With a hacksaw, cut four dowels the same height. Place dowels inside the dots marked.

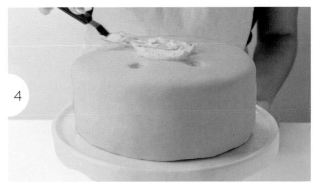

4 Spread a layer of icing in the center of the cake. Place on top layer, using the dots marked from the Smart Marker as a guide. Add a border if desired.

cake chart

The numbers and quantities in the following chart are provided as an estimate and are meant to be used as a general guide. Requirements and results will vary according to the user.

SHEET CAKES	NUMBER OF SERVINGS	CAKE BATTER NEEDED	FILLING NEEDED	ICING NEEDED	FONDANT NEEDED
9" x 13" (23 x 33 cm) (quarter sheet cake)	20	6 cups (1.5 L)	1½ cups (375 mL)	6 cups (1.5 L)	40 ounces (1 kg)
11" x 15" (28 x 38 cm)	25	10 cups (2.3 L)	2½ cups (625 mL)	8 cups (2 L)	60 ounces (1.7 kg)
12" x 18" (30 x 46 cm) (half sheet cake)	36	13 cups (3 L)	3½ cups (875 mL)	10 cups (2.3 L)	80 ounces (2.2 kg)

ROUND CAKES	NUMBER OF SERVINGS	CAKE BATTER NEEDED	FILLING NEEDED	ICING NEEDED	FONDANT NEEDED
6" (15 cm)	8	1¼ cups (300 mL)	⅓ cups (75 mL)	3 cups (750 mL)	18 ounces (0.5 kg)
7" (18 cm)	10	1¾ cups (425 mL)	⅔ cups (150 mL)	3½ cups (875 mL)	21 ounces (0.6 kg)
8" (20 cm)	18	2½ cups (625 mL)	¾ cups (175 mL)	4½ cups (1.125 L)	24 ounces (0.7 kg)
9" (23 cm)	24	2¾ cups (675 mL)	1 cup (250 mL)	5 cups (1.25 L)	30 ounces (0.9 kg)
10" (25 cm)	28	4¼ cups (1 L)	1¼ cups (300 mL)	5½ cups (1.375 L)	36 ounces (1 kg)
12" (30 cm)	40	5½ cups (1.4 L)	1¾ cups (425 mL)	6½ cups (1.6 L)	48 ounces (1.3 kg)
14" (36 cm)	64	7½ cups (1.8 L)	2½ cups (625 mL)	7¾ cups (1.9 L)	72 ounces (2 kg)
16" (40 cm)	80	11 cups (2.6 L)	3⅔ cups (900 mL)	9¼ cups (2.3 L)	108 ounces (3 kg)
18" (46 cm)	110	15 cups (3.5 L)	5⅔ cups (1.4 L)	11 cups (2.6 L)	140 ounces (3.9 kg)

SQUARE CAKES	NUMBER OF SERVINGS	CAKE BATTER NEEDED	FILLING NEEDED	ICING NEEDED	FONDANT NEEDED
6" (15 cm)	12	2¼ cups (550 mL)	¾ cup (175 mL)	4 cups (1 L)	24 ounces (0.7 kg)
7" (18 cm)	16	3½ cups (875 mL)	⅔ cup (150 mL)	4¾ cups (1.2 L)	30 ounces (0.9 kg)
8" (20 cm)	22	4 cups (1 L)	1 cup (250 mL)	5 cups (1.25 L)	36 ounces (1 kg)
9" (23 cm)	25	5½ cups (1.375 L)	1¼ cup (300 mL)	5¾ cups (1.4 L)	42 ounces (1.1 kg)
10" (25 cm)	35	7 cups (1.75 L)	1½ cup (375 mL)	6½ cups (1.6 L)	48 ounces (1.3 kg)
12" (30 cm)	50	10 cups (2.3 L)	2 cups (500 mL)	8 cups (2 L)	72 ounces (2 kg)
14" (36 cm)	75	14 cups (3.5 L)	3 cups (750 mL)	9¾ cups (2.5 L)	96 ounces (2.7 kg)
16" (40 cm)	100	18 cups (4.2 L)	4½ cups (1.125 L)	11¾ cups (2.9 L)	120 ounces (3.4 kg)

BAKE TEMP	BAKE TIME
350°F (175°C)	35-40 min
325°F (160°C)	35-40 min
325°F (160°C)	45-50 min

BAKE TEMP	BAKE TIME
350°F (175°C)	25-30 min
350°F (175°C)	23-32 min
350°F (175°C)	30-35 min
350°F (175°C)	30-35 min
350°F (175°C)	35-40 min
350°F (175°C)	35-40 min
325°F (160°C)	50-55 min
325°F (160°C)	55-60 min
325°F (160°C)	60-65 min

BAKE TEMP	BAKE TIME
350°F (175°C)	25-30 min
350°F (175°C)	25-32 min
350°F (175°C)	35-40 min
350°F (175°C)	35-40 min
350°F (175°C)	35-40 min
350°F (175°C)	40-45 min
350°F (175°C)	45-50 min
325°F (160°C)	45-50 min

NUMBER OF SERVINGS

The number of servings will depend entirely on how large or how small the cake is cut. For example a 12" × 18" (30 × 46 cm) sheet cake will serve 54 if the pieces are cut into 2" × 2" (5 × 5 cm) squares, or 36 if the pieces are cut into 2" × 3" (5 × 7.5 cm) rectangles. The number of servings for the sheet cake is based on a one-layer cake. The number of servings for round and square cakes is based on a two-layer cake. When figuring the size of cake to bake, bigger is better. It is better to err with extra cake than to run out of cake.

CAKE BATTER

One standard cake mix contains four to six cups (1 L to 1.5 L) of batter. The charts for the amount of batter needed are based on filling a single pan that is 2" (5 cm) tall, filling ⅔ full with cake batter. Filling the pan with less than ⅔ batter may produce a cake that is too thin.

FILLINGS

The amount of filling needed may fluctuate depending on the type of filling used. The cake charts are based on a thin layer of pastry filling. If a thick, fluffy filling will be used, such as buttercream, the amount of filling required should be doubled.

ICING

The amount of icing needed is based on icing the cake with the buttercream icing recipe included in this book. The amount of icing needed will vary according to consistency, thickness applied, or if other recipes are used. The figures for the amount of icing needed include enough icing for piping a border or simple piped accents. The amount of icing needed for the sheet cake is based on a one-layer cake. The amount of icing needed for the square and round cake is based on a two-layer cake.

ROLLED FONDANT

The figure for the amount of fondant needed includes just the amount needed for covering the cake and does not include additional decorations. This amount can vary significantly depending on the thickness of the rolled fondant.

PIPING TECHNIQUES

Learning how to fill pastry bags, hold pastry bags, and pipe simple shapes are fundamental skills of cake decorating. This section covers an abundance of basic piping techniques including flowers, borders, and writing. More intricate cake decorating techniques are given for the most special of occasions. The advanced decorating technique called brush embroidery is also included.

using pastry bags, tips, and couplers

Tips may be dropped into the bag without a coupler, or a coupler may be used to change tips without filling a new bag.

FITTING A BAG WITH A COUPLER

1 Cut the reusable pastry bag or disposable pastry bag so that one or two threads are showing on the coupler base when the coupler base is dropped into the bag. Pull the coupler tightly to secure.

2 Place tip on the coupler base.

3 Twist the coupler screw top to tighten the tip in place.

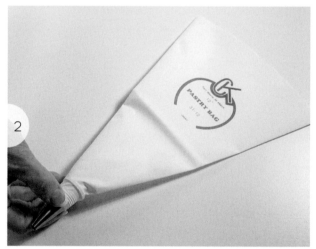

FILLING REUSABLE AND DISPOSABLE PASTRY BAGS

1 Drop the tip into the pastry bag and tug on the end to secure. The bag may also be fitted with a coupler following instructions opposite. Fold the pastry bag over hands to form a cuff. The cuff fold should be 2" to 3" (5 to 7.5 cm).

2 Scoop icing into the bag until it reaches the top of the cuff. Fill the bag about half full with icing. The more full the bag, the more difficult the bag is to control.

3 Unfold the cuff. Squeeze the bag between thumb and fingers and push the icing toward the bottom of the bag.

4 Twist the bag where the icing begins. For more security, secure with a rubber band or icing bag tie to prevent the icing from bursting from the top of the bag.

REFILLING

Each time pastry bags are refilled, there is a build-up of air. Before beginning to pipe again, squeeze the pastry bag to release trapped air; otherwise a large air bubble will interrupt the piping.

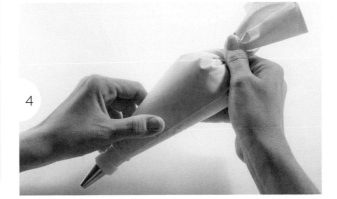

MAKING A PARCHMENT CONE

Parchment paper is available in precut triangles. These triangles are formed to create pastry bags that are lightweight, inexpensive, and disposable. If a parchment cone is well made, a tip may not be needed when a round opening is desired. Simply cut the tapered end of the parchment cone to the size needed.

1 The triangle is labeled A, B, and C.

2 Fold corner A to meet corner B, twisting to form a cone.

3 Fold corner C to meet corner B, keeping the cone shape with a tight point. Align all three points.

4 Cross over corners A and C, making a "W" to ensure the seams of the cone overlap. Always keep the bottom point tight. Shift A and C up and down to assure a tight point. Fold in the W-shaped corners of the bag. Cut the parchment bag at the point, large enough so one-third of a tip will protrude from the bag. Drop the tip into the bag. If more than one-third of the tip is showing, it may pop out during piping.

TAPE IT

The seam of the parchment bag can be secured with tape if you have difficulty maintaining a fine point while filling the bag.

FILLING PARCHMENT CONES

1 Hold the parchment bag and fill half-full with icing. Squeeze the bag between your thumb and fingers to fill the bottom of the bag.

2 Fold in the left side, then the right side. Fold down the middle, and continue to fold until you reach the top of the icing.

HOLDING THE BAG

The most common angles to hold a bag are $45°$ and $90°$. To control the icing, grip and squeeze the bag with dominant hand. Use the index finger of the nondominant hand to guide the bag.

3 The $90°$ angle is commonly used for piping stars, balls, some flowers, and figure piping.

4 A $45°$ angle is commonly used for borders, writing, several flowers, and side designs.

5 The amount of pressure applied is a key factor for successful piping. The amount of pressure may vary depending on what is piped, but in most cases, it is important to have consistent pressure. Shown are piped dots using a #10 tip with small, medium, and large amounts of pressure.

PREVENT DRYING

When not in use, the icing in the tips of filled pastry bags can become hard and crusted. Keep the filled pastry bags covered with a damp cloth or with a tip cover when not in use.

tip usage

Tips are available in a few finishes. Stainless steel tips provide details with sharp, crisp lines. Precise plastic tips are an alternative to metal tips, which may rust. Wash the tips with a tip cleaning brush. Thoroughly dry each tip after washing to keep tips from rusting. Be sure to purchase tips that do not have a seam to keep the piping defined. English tips, such as PME Supatubes, have numbers that do not correspond to U.S. tip numbers. The supatubes are precise, stainless steel tips.

ROUND TIPS

Round tips are used in a variety of piping. Round openings are used for lines, stems, cornelli (a pattern of random, continuous squiggles), swirls, dots, balls, writing, stringwork, lacework, figure piping, run sugar pictures, flower centers, and dot borders. Large round tips, such as #2A and #1A are used to quickly and neatly apply icing to tops of cupcakes. Round tips are used so frequently, it is practical to have nearly every size of round opening available.

When using tips with a tiny opening, it is important to sift the powdered sugar. Use a sifter with a very fine mesh. If the tips get clogged, a straight pin can unclog the tip, but pins may also damage the tip. Unclogging the tip with a straight pin also only serves as a temporary solution. The piece that was clogging the tip will be pushed back into the icing and likely return.

STAR TIPS

Star tips are used for many borders, star flowers, rosettes, and filling in a shaped cake. They are available in open star or closed star. The prongs of the star tips can be damaged and bent easily.

Use care when washing and storing to prevent the prongs from bending. A large star tip, such as tip #1G or #1M is used for piping icing in a decorative design on top of cupcakes.

DROP FLOWER TIPS

Drop flower tips look similar to a star, but the center has a post. The post creates flowers with an empty center and full and detailed petals.

LEAF TIPS

Leaf tips are used to pipe petals, leaves, and poinsettias. Leaf tips with a V shape, such as #352 and #366, work well for piping leaves with a fine point.

PETAL AND RUFFLE TIPS

Petal and ruffle tips have a long teardrop shape that produces lovely rose petals, fan petals, carnations, and simple ruffles. Variations of the petal tips include a curved rose petal tip and an S-shape rose petal tip.

MISCELLANEOUS TIPS

Several other shapes are available for a variety of uses, for example, tips with several round openings can be used for music bar lines. Chrysanthemum tips have a U shape to create long, cupped petals. Specialty-use tips that are handy to have on hand include the quick icer tip #789 and the bismark tip #230 for filling cupcakes.

Many companies have tip kits with a variety of sizes and designs. The kits can range from three or four tips up to a hundred tips. The tips on the opposite page would make a nice beginning set.

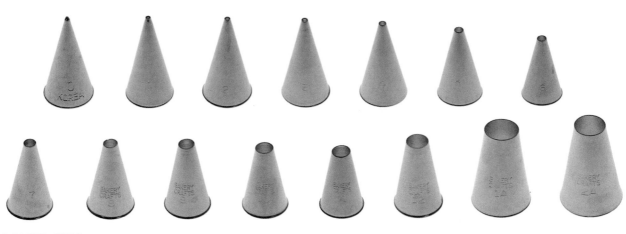

ROUND TIPS
#0-12, #1A, and #2A

STAR TIPS
#16, #21, #32, #199, and #1M

DROP FLOWER TIPS
#129, #131, and #190

LEAF TIPS
#349, #352, and #366

PETAL TIPS
#102, #103, and #104

BASKETWEAVE TIP
#47

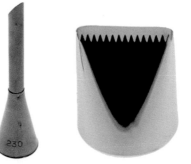

MISCELLANEOUS TIPS
Bismark #230, Quick icer #789

basic piping

It is important to keep the tip clean and free of built up icing for crisp and precise piping. The instructions here use standard tip sizes.

BALL

A ball can be used for a simple border, flower center, figure piping, and piped dots.

1 Start with the pastry bag at a 90° angle, just above the surface. Squeeze the pastry bag to pipe a dot, holding the tip steady as the icing forms around the tip. Continue squeezing the pastry bag until the dot is the desired size. Stop pressure and lift pastry bag.

2 If there are small peaks after the dots are formed, gently press the peak with the tip of index finger just before the icing forms a crust.

STARS

Stars are used to create simple piped accents or flowers. Pipe a small dot in the center of the star for a flower. The opening of the star tip should determine the size of the piped star. Stars are also commonly used on shaped cakes baked in molds and are piped closely together to completely cover the cake.

3 Start with the pastry bag at a 90° angle, just above the surface. Squeeze the pastry bag.

4 Continue squeezing the pastry bag until the star is the desired size. The bag should not be lifted until the star is formed. Stop pressure and lift pastry bag. When piping stars side by side, pipe them close together so that there are no gaps.

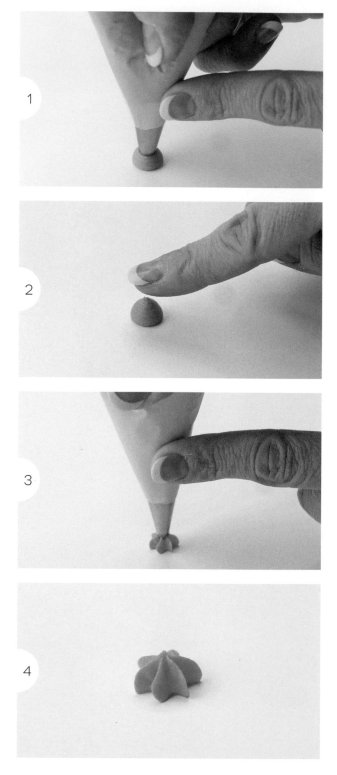

LEAVES

The shape of the tip, how you hold it, and how long you make the leaves all affect their appearance.

1 Position the pastry bag at a 45° angle. One point of the tip should be touching the surface.

2 Squeeze the pastry bag with a short burst of pressure to attach leaf. Gradually release pressure and lift the tip. Stop pressure and lift pastry bag.

3 To give a leaf a ruffled texture, move the bag up and down slightly while squeezing.

4 Leaves can be made in a variety of lengths using the same size tip. Pull the tip while applying steady pressure for an elongated leaf.

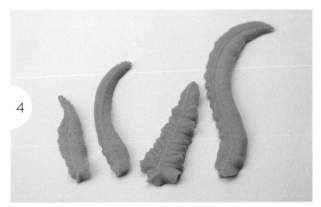

FUR/HAIR/SIDE-VIEW GRASS

1 Position the pastry bag at a 45° angle. The tip should be touching the surface. Squeeze the pastry bag with a short burst of pressure to attach fur.

2 Continue with pressure and drag the tip to desired length. Stop pressure and lift pastry bag.

3 Pipe a row of adjoining fur close together so there are no gaps.

4 If piping fur, start at the bottom of the cake and pipe a row of fur. Start the next row slightly above and drag the icing to overlap the starting point of the previous row.

KEEP IT CLEAN

For detailed icing strands, it is important to keep the tip clean. Most metal grass tips have ridges around the fine holes. The ridges make it difficult to keep the end of the metal tip clean. The plastic grass tip is smooth without ridges, which makes it easier to keep clean.

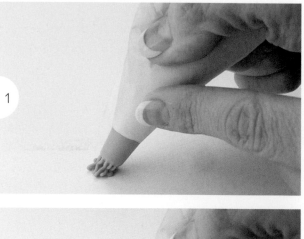

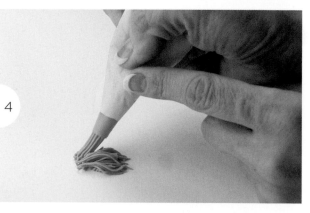

GRASS

1 Position the pastry bag at a 90° angle. The tip should be touching the surface. Squeeze the pastry bag with a short burst of pressure to attach grass.

2 Continue with pressure and drag the tip upward. Stop pressure and lift pastry bag. Pipe the grass close together so there are no gaps.

3 The length and style of grass can vary. To pipe long strands of grass, attach grass with a burst of pressure. Continue with a lot of pressure while lifting for long grass.

SWIRLS/FINE LINES

A round tip opening is used to pipe lines, swirls, and stems.

4 Position the pastry bag at a 45° angle. Squeeze the pastry bag to release icing, touch surface, then lift icing just above surface continuing with pressure.

5 Continue piping with uninterrupted pressure piping the lines or swirls. Let the icing flow from the bag naturally just above surface. Do not drag the tip on the cake. Stop pressure and touch the surface to attach the end of the swirl.

PRESSURE

If too much pressure is applied, the lines may have wiggles or loops. If lines break when piping, not enough pressure is being applied or the piping bag is moving too fast.

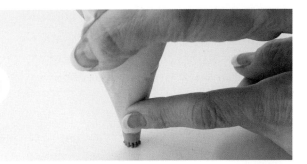

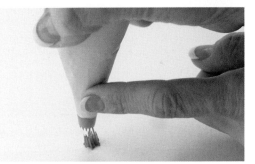

BASKETWEAVE

A cake piped using a basketweave tip gives a pretty woven effect. A star tip can also be used for piping basketweave.

1 Pipe a vertical line the height of the area covered. Then pipe short, horizontal lines over the vertical line, allowing a space the width of the tip between each horizontal line.

2 Cover ends of the horizontal line with another vertical line.

3 Start the next group of horizontal lines in the empty space, holding the tip against the first vertical line. Cross over the second vertical line. Repeat until the area is finished.

4 The design of the basketweave is changed by the tip style. The basketweave in image 4 is piped using a #16 star tip.

5 Some basketweave tips are ridged on both sides, while other basketweave tips have a smooth side and a ridged side. Shown in image 5 is tip #47. The smooth side of the tip is used for the vertical lines while the ridged side of the tip is used for the horizontal lines.

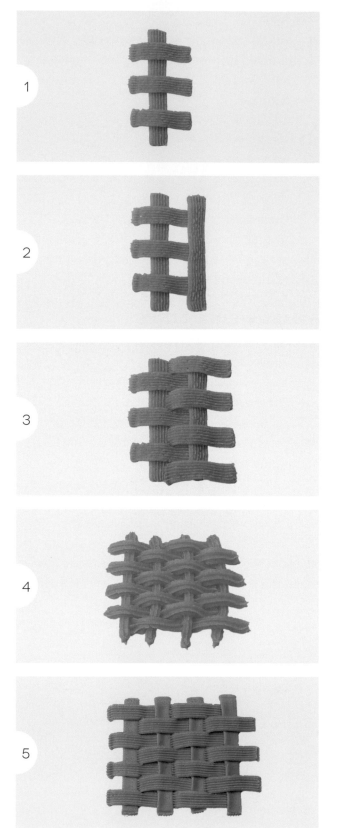

1

2

3

4

5

RUFFLES

1 Place the wide end of the rose petal tip against the cake with the narrow end slightly angled up from the cake.

2 Apply pressure.

3 Continue with pressure, keeping the wide end of the rose tip touching the cake, and move wrist up and down to curl the icing.

4 Continue the ruffle around the cake. The ruffle can be piped as a swag by curving the garland.

PREVENT CLOGGING

Fine tips, such as tip #1, are easily clogged. When mixing royal icing, make sure the powdered sugar is thoroughly sifted to avoid clumps. If the tips should get clogged, use a straight pin to carefully unclog the tip.

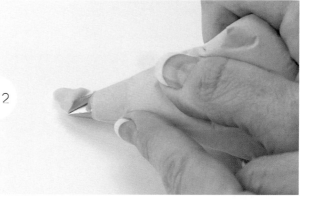

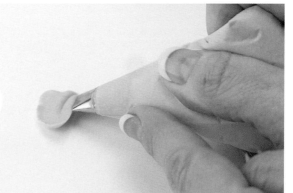

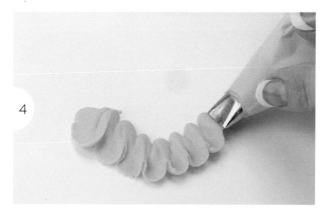

PIPED BORDERS

Piped borders give cakes a finished, professional look. Placing the cake on a turntable allows the cake to revolve for an even, consistent border. For a round cake, start piping at 3:00. When piping borders on a sheet cake, start at one corner. Move hand along the side of the cake with steady, even pressure.

The size and shape of each border will vary depending on the tip. The borders shown here are piped using common sizes of decorating tips. For daintier border designs, use smaller opening tips. View the tip guide on page 45 for ideas on the shape and size each tip will provide.

Practice achieving consistent pressure on the back of a flat baking pan before piping directly on the cake.

DOT BORDER

Dots add a clean, simple border to cakes. A dot is made by using a tip with a round opening. Shown is tip #10.

1 Start with the pastry bag at a 90° angle, just above the surface.

2 Squeeze the pastry bag to pipe a dot, holding the tip steady. Continue squeezing the pastry bag until the dot is the desired size. Stop pressure and lift pastry bag.

3 Continue piping dots side by side, keeping the pressure consistent.

4 If there are small peaks on the dots, gently press the peak with the index finger just before the icing completely forms a crust.

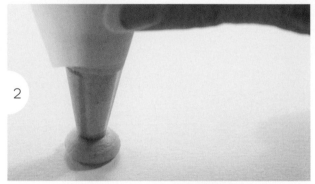

STAR BORDER

This border is piped exactly like the dot border. The stars are formed using a star tip. Shown is tip #18.

1 Start with the pastry bag at a 90° angle, just above the surface.

2 Squeeze the pastry bag to pipe a star.

3 Continue squeezing the pastry bag until the star is the desired size. The bag should not be lifted until the star is formed. Stop pressure and lift pastry bag.

4 Continue piping stars side by side, keeping the pressure consistent.

TEARDROP BORDER

A teardrop border is formed by using a round tip and piping a row of attached teardrops. Shown is tip #10.

1 Position the pastry bag at a 45° angle, nearly touching the surface. Squeeze the pastry bag to form a ball.

2 Gradually release pressure and drag the tip to form a teardrop. Stop pressure and lift pastry bag.

3 Start the next teardrop at the end of the first teardrop.

4 Continue piping teardrops, keeping the pressure consistent.

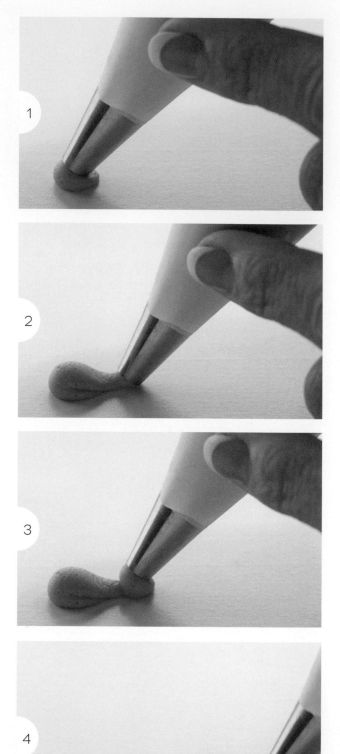

SHELL BORDER

A shell border is one of the most popular borders in cake decorating. It is made by piping a series of shells in a row using a star tip. Shown is tip #18.

1 Position the pastry bag at a 45° angle, nearly touching the surface. Apply pressure while moving the tip forward slightly.

2 Move back to the starting point, gradually release pressure, and drag the tip to form a shell. Stop pressure and pull tip away.

3 Start the next shell at the tail of the first shell and continue piping shells until the border is complete.

ZIG-ZAG BORDER

Use a star tip to pipe this classic border. This border can vary in design by piping the points close together, or by stretching the distance between the points. Shown is tip #18.

4 Position the pastry bag at a 45° angle, nearly touching the surface. With steady pressure move the tip in a zig-zag pattern. When border is complete, stop pressure and lift pastry bag.

ROPE BORDER

A rope border complements western-themed cakes. It is also a lovely border for piped basketweave. Pipe the rope border with a star tip. Shown is tip #18.

1 Position the pastry bag at a 45° angle, nearly touching the surface. Pipe a U shape using steady pressure.

2 Insert end of tip into the curve of the piped U shape, holding the bag away from the U.

3 Apply minimal pressure, pull tip down, then lift icing over endpoint of U and form next U.

4 Repeat steps 2 and 3 until border is complete.

QUESTION MARK BORDER

The question mark border is an elegant border using a star tip. This border design can have different looks by piping the sideways question marks closer together or farther apart. Shown is tip #18.

1 Hold the pastry bag at a 45° angle, nearly touching the surface. Attach icing with a burst of pressure.

2 Continue with light pressure and pipe a sideways question mark, ending with a curved tail. Do not release pressure.

3 Continue pressure, slightly backing into the curve of the first tail; then move forward to form the next sideways question mark.

4 Continue piping until border is complete.

C-BORDER

The C-border is piped the same as the question mark border, but in reverse. This border design can vary by piping the sideways C-shape closer together or farther apart.

1 Hold the pastry bag at a 45° angle, nearly touching the surface.

2 Attach icing with a burst of pressure.

3 Continue with light pressure and pipe a sideways C shape, ending with a curved tail. Do not release pressure.

4 Continue pressure, slightly backing into the curve of the first tail; then move forward to form the next sideways C shape. Continue piping until border is complete.

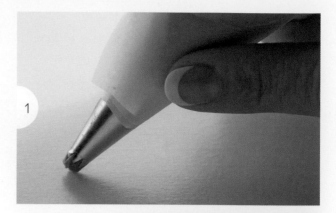

REVERSE SCROLL BORDER

The reverse scroll border is piped with a star tip and combines the C-border with the question mark border. Shown is tip #18.

1 Hold the pastry bag at a 45° angle, nearly touching the surface.

2 Attach icing with a burst of pressure and pipe a sideways C shape, ending with a curved tail. Do not release pressure.

3 Continue pressure, slightly backing into the curve of the first tail; then move forward to form a sideways question mark ending with a curved tail.

4 Alternate the C shape and question mark designs to complete the border.

WRITING

Mastering writing takes practice. Ensure perfect letting with a pattern press transfer method. It is best to allow buttercream icing to crust completely before piping letters or the coloring may bleed. When possible, pipe the writing on the cake before adding additional decoration. This allows you to add the flowers and accents around the letters. Use a #1 or a #2 tip for fine writing. Larger round openings may be used, but letters may look undefined.

PIPING LETTERS

1 Position the pastry bag at a 45° angle, touching the surface. Squeeze icing while lifting the bag just above the surface.

2 Continue with steady pressure and pipe the letter. Let the icing flow from the bag naturally just above surface. Do not drag the tip on the cake.

3 Touch surface and stop squeezing.

PERFECT PENMANSHIP

* The icing can be thinned slightly with a few drops of water.

* On a freshly covered fondant cake, or after the buttercream has crusted, use a ruler and toothpick to mark dots on the icing to make a straight line to follow.

* Practice on a sheet of parchment paper to know how much area the message needs.

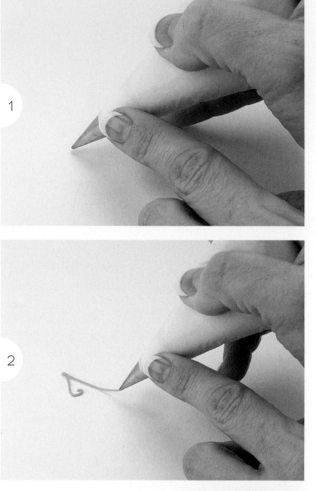

PATTERN PRESSES

Pattern presses are available in a variety of sayings, or you can write your own with alphabet presses.

1 Press letters into cake.

2 Lift pattern press.

3 Pipe on top of the embossed letters.

For Buttercream

It is important to allow the buttercream to crust completely before pressing the pattern into the icing.

For Rolled Fondant

It is important to emboss the rolled fondant soon after the cake is covered, or the rolled fondant will crack when the letters are pushed into it.

4 Another technique is to saturate a dry felt pad with airbrush color. Rub the letters against the saturated pad. Emboss the rolled fondant with the letters. Practice on a scrap piece of rolled fondant before embossing the covered cake.

SIMPLE FLOWERS

These flowers are easy to pipe, dainty, and work well as fillers. The flowers can be piped directly onto the cake when using buttercream. Pipe royal icing flowers on parchment paper and allow to set for several hours. When hardened, put in a container and store up to several months.

STAR FLOWERS

1 Start with the pastry bag at a 90° angle touching the surface. Squeeze the pastry bag to pipe a star and continue squeezing until the star is the desired size. The bag should not be lifted until the star is formed. Stop pressure and lift pastry bag.

2 Use a contrasting color and pipe a dot in the center.

DROP FLOWERS

3 Start with the pastry bag at a 90° angle, touching the surface. Keep the tip touching the surface and apply pressure while turning the tip a quarter turn. Release pressure and raise tip straight up with a slight jerk to break off icing.

4 Use a contrasting color and pipe a dot in the center.

DEFINED PETALS

For defined petals, apply pressure and turn at the same time. For ruffled flowers (shown), use stiff buttercream. For smooth petals, thin the buttercream slightly with water.

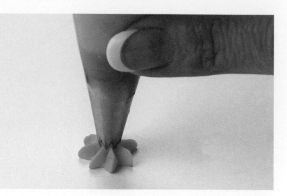

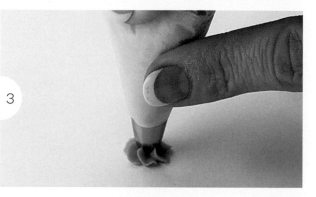

ADVANCED FLOWERS

The instructions here are for flowers made with buttercream icing. Most flowers may also be made with royal icing. Buttercream flowers may be made a few days ahead of time. Royal icing flowers may be made months ahead of time. Store flowers at room temperature in a loosely covered box. When mixing buttercream icing or royal icing from scratch, add less water if desiring a stiffer icing. If the buttercream icing or royal icing is already prepared, additional powdered sugar may be added. Flowers with smooth edges require a medium consistency icing. If the petals are too rough, add a bit of water to the buttercream or royal icing; too much water will cause the petals to collapse or run together.

USING A FLOWER NAIL

A flower nail is used as a mini turntable controlled by fingers to make the flow of the icing consistent.

1 Add a dot of icing on the nail. Attach a small square of parchment paper.

2 Hold flower nail with index finger and thumb. Twirl the nail so that the nail turns naturally. Pipe desired flower.

3 Slide parchment square onto a tray and allow flowers to dry. When the flowers are dry, slide a spatula with a thin blade under the flower to release. Transfer the flower to the cake.

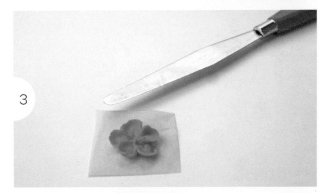

4 If flowers are going to be used immediately, they can be piped directly onto the nail, and removed with a flower lifter or thin spatula.

ROSES

1 Fit a pastry bag with a coupler and fill with icing. Hold the pastry bag at a 90° angle, lightly touching the surface. Apply heavy pressure, then decrease pressure while lifting to form a cone.

2 Attach tip #104 to the coupler. Begin turning the nail. With the wide end of the rose tip facing down, gently press tip into the cone. Start about halfway down on the cone and form a spiral. Continue turning the nail and form an additional spiral just above the first.

3 Continue with pressure, and drag the end of the spiral toward the base of the cone. Stop pressure and lift tip.

4 Turn the nail and form a petal. The petal is formed by gently pushing the wide end of the tip into the cone and forming an arch. The top of the petal should be nearly as tall as the center cone. Start the second petal overlapping the first.

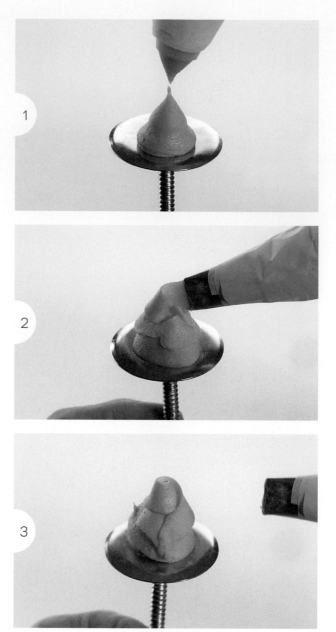

MAKING ROSES

When forming a rose, the nail should determine the forward and backward motion of the petals. Do not move the tip back and forth; only move it up and down.

5 Pipe a third petal overlapping the second. The rose should now have three overlapping petals.

6 Make five additional petals, starting at the base with the wide end of the tip down and the narrow end of the tip slightly tipped outward.

7 Continue turning the nail and forming petals. Each petal should overlap.

8 A traditional piped rose has three inner petals, five middle petals, and seven outer petals.

ROSEBUDS

1 Fit a pastry bag with a #103 tip and fill with icing. Start with the pastry bag at a 45° angle, with the wide end of the rose tip lightly touching the surface. Apply a burst of pressure to attach icing. Continue pressure while moving tip slightly to the left. Continue pressure and move tip slightly to the right. Release pressure and pull away sharply to break off. This will make the base of the rosebud. The rosebud base should be a cone shape with a slight crevice.

2 Hold the tip just above the work surface. Insert tip into the crevice of the cone. Apply pressure and pull away from the rosebud approximately ¼" (6 mm).

3 Continue with pressure and come back to the center of the rosebud. Gently touch the rosebud. Stop pressure and pull away.

4 Fill a pastry bag with green icing and a #2 tip. Start at the base of the rosebud and apply a burst of pressure. Continue with pressure and pipe a stem. Add sepals around the base of the rosebud. Fill a pastry bag with green icing and a #349 leaf tip. Add leaves to the stem.

The rosebud should be hollow inside, made by creating a crevice in step one and folding over the crevice in steps two and three.

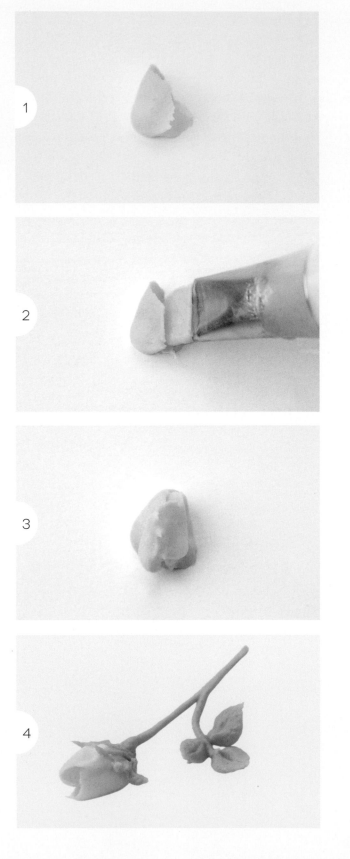

CARNATIONS

1 Fit a pastry bag with a #103 tip and fill with stiff icing. Attach a square of parchment paper to the nail with a small amount of icing. Hold the pastry bag at a 45° angle, with the wide end of the rose tip touching the nail. Move wrists rapidly up and down to make a circle of tiny, ruffled petals around the edge of the nail.

2 Make a second row of ruffled petals just inside the first row. The second row should be angled up slightly and shorter than the first row.

3 Starting in the center, add a third row of very short, ruffled petals.

4 Add additional short, standing ruffled petals to fill in the center.

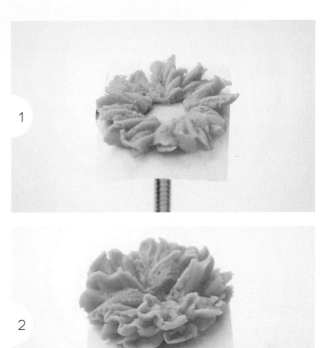

CHRYSANTHEMUMS

1 Fit a pastry bag with a coupler and fill with icing. Do not add a decorating tip or coupler ring. Attach a square of parchment paper to the nail with a small amount of icing. Pipe a ball of icing in the center of the nail.

2 Attach tip #81 to the coupler. Insert tip into the ball of icing with the curved part of the tip resting on the nail. Apply pressure and pull tip toward the edge of the nail. Stop pressure and pull away to detach. Continue piping petals around the ball. The petals should be close together.

3 Pipe a row of petals just above the first layer. These petals should be shorter and the petals should be angled slightly more than the first layer. Continue piping rows of petals. Each row of petals should be shorter and angle up slightly more than the previous row.

4 The center petals should be standing straight up.

APPLE BLOSSOMS

1 Fit a pastry bag with a #102 tip and fill with icing. Attach a square of parchment paper to the nail with a small amount of icing. Hold the pastry bag with the wide end of the rose tip touching the nail.

2 Rest the wide end of the tip in the center of the nail. The narrow end should be angled slightly above the nail. Slowly turning the nail, apply pressure and move the tip ⅜" (1 cm) toward the edge of the nail. Turn the nail slightly to curve the petal. With continuous pressure, curve the petal and return to the center following the ⅜" (1 cm) line. When piping fan petals, the angle should not change and the wide end should always touch the nail. The shape of each petal should be a teardrop not an arch.

3 Pipe four more petals the same way, starting each petal under the previously piped petal.

4 Pipe dots in the flower center with tip #1.

5 Variations of this flower may be made in an assortment of sizes, colors, and centers.

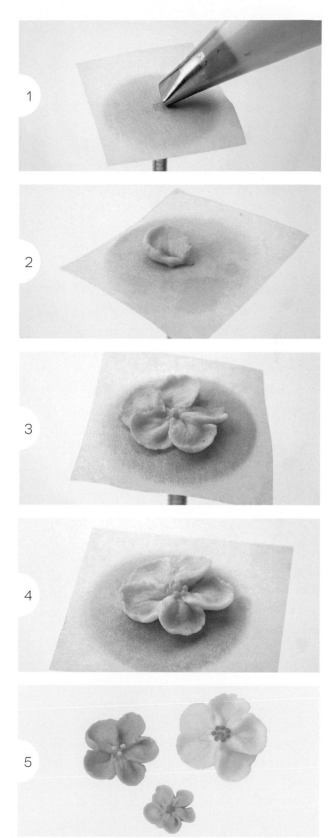

DAISIES

1 Fit a pastry bag with a #101S tip and fill with icing. Attach a square of parchment paper to the nail with a small amount of icing. Pipe a dot in the center of the nail as a center guide when forming the petals.

Rest the wide end of the tip in the center of the nail. The narrow end should be angled slightly above the nail. Apply pressure and move the tip ½" (1.3 cm) toward the edge of the nail. Turn the nail slightly to curve the petal. With continuous pressure, curve the petal and return to the center following the ½" (1.3 cm) line, piping a long fan petal. When piping fan petals, the angle should not change and the wide end should always touch the nail.

2 Continue piping the petals close together, so that each ends at the center. Each petal should be piped slightly over the previously piped petal.

3 Pipe the remaining petals. When piping the last petal, start under the first petal piped, and end on top of the previous piped petal.

4 Fill a pastry bag with icing and a #233 tip. Hold tip #233 at a 90° angle in the center of the daisy. Squeeze icing bag with a burst of pressure. Stop pressure and pull away. Allow the peaks of the daisy center to crust, then soften peaks with finger.

SMOOTH EDGES

If the petals have rough edges, thin the buttercream icing slightly with water. Be careful not to add much water, or the petals will run together.

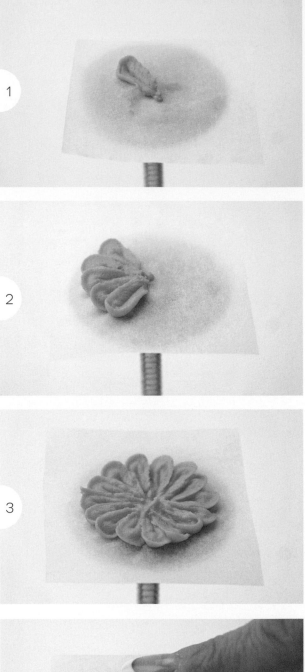

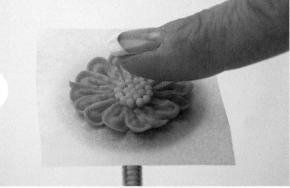

BRUSH EMBROIDERY

Brush embroidery adds a delicate lace texture to fondant-covered cakes. It is created by outlining flower petals with royal icing, then brushing the icing before it hardens. The background color should show through toward the center.

The rolled fondant must be soft when pressing cutters into it. To keep the fondant soft, wrap the fondant-covered cake with plastic wrap immediately after the cake is iced. Unwrap small sections of the cake and emboss.

The brush should be clean and damp. Keep a bowl of water to rinse the brush after every petal is decorated. Wipe off excess water with a damp towel. The brushed icing should be thick where the outline starts and thin toward the center. Brush strokes should be visible—if not, the royal icing is too thin. Add more powdered sugar and whip until stiff peaks form.

1 Immediately after the cake is covered with rolled fondant, emboss it with flower cutters.

2 Place royal icing in a pastry bag with a round tip. For flowers and leaves sized 2" to 4" (5 to 10 cm), use tip #3. Use tip #1 or #2 for smaller flowers and leaves. Outline one petal with royal icing.

3 Gently touch the top of the outline with a damp, flat brush. Hold the brush at a 45° angle. With long strokes, drag the royal icing from the outline to the center. Repeat, outlining and brushing one petal at a time. The royal icing may harden if too many petals are outlined at once.

4 Add a center to the flowers or veins to the leaves with royal icing and a #1 tip.

FONDANT AND GUM PASTE ACCENTS

Even beginners can create professional looking cakes using rolled fondant for cutting, sculpting, and shaping beautiful accents. Most accents shown throughout this section can be placed on buttercream or fondant-covered cakes. Adorn a cake with simple, cut fondant flowers or with an elaborate gum paste rose bouquet. In many cases, rolled fondant or gum paste may be used interchangeably or a 50/50 blend may be used. If the accent piece is likely to be eaten, it should be made from rolled fondant. If it is for decoration, use gum paste for a thinner, more delicate piece. If gum paste is best suited for the accent piece, it will be stated in the instructions.

essential equiptment

PASTA MACHINE

A pasta machine is not mandatory for success, but is very useful in maintaining consistent thickness when rolling fondant and gum paste. Because a pasta machine will not make the paste wider, only longer, be sure to start with paste the width you need. If a piece of paste needs to be wider than the pasta machine barrel, roll freehand and use a rolling pin with rings or perfection strips. A fondant sheeter is available for large pieces.

If the paste is not completely smooth after it has been fed through the machine, there may be residue on the roller. Clean and thoroughly dry the roller after each use.

1 Knead and soften gum paste or rolled fondant. Roll the width needed. Set the pasta machine to the thickest setting and insert the paste. Activate the machine and take hold of the paste with your hands as it is fed through.

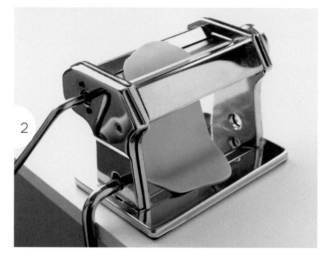

2 Turn the setting to the next thinner setting and feed the paste again.

3 Continue feeding the paste and turn the dial to a thinner setting between each roll.

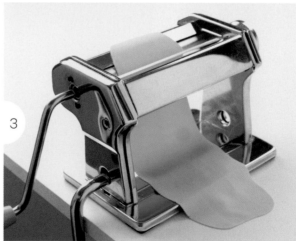

THIN GRADUALLY

Usually the paste can be thinned by rolling every other setting. If there are wrinkles in the paste or the paste is not completely smooth, do not skip a setting.

CLAY EXTRUDER

A clay extruder is used to create a variety of lines, textures, and details with consistent thickness. The extruder kits include an assortment of interchangeable disks.

1 Knead and soften rolled fondant or gum paste. Roll a cylinder of paste the length of the extruder and slightly smaller in diameter than the extruder barrel. Feed the barrel of the extruder from the bottom.

2 Choose the desired disk and attach to the extruder.

3 Twist the handle on the gun to release the paste.

4 Use a paring knife or a spatula with a thin blade to cut extruded paste.

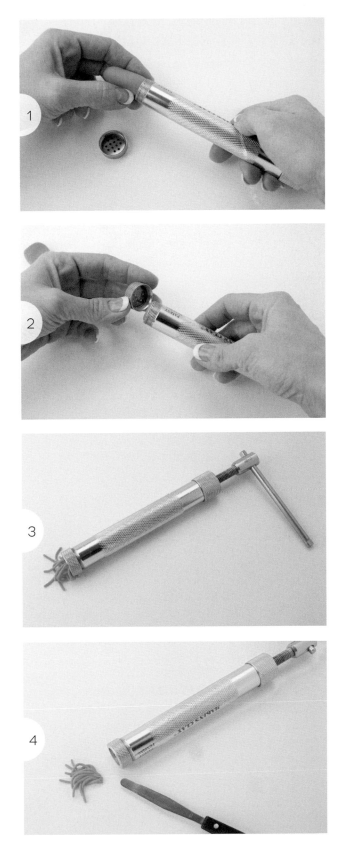

PASTE ACCENTS MADE WITH CLAY EXTRUDER

1 Single round openings are used for vines, stems, letters, and borders.

2 Multiple round openings are used for hair, straw, flower stamens, and fur.

3 Flat disks are used for ribbons around the side of the cake, baskets, and bows.

4 The clovers and hexagons are used for making ropes. Clovers give the most striking twist design.

5 Additional disks are included with most sets for more designs.

6 Combine colors for a multicolored rope.

SLIGHT WARMING

If you are struggling to release the paste from the extruder, try warming the paste. Remove the paste cylinder from the extruder, and place it in the microwave for 2 or 3 seconds, or until just warm. Put the paste back into the extruder and try again.

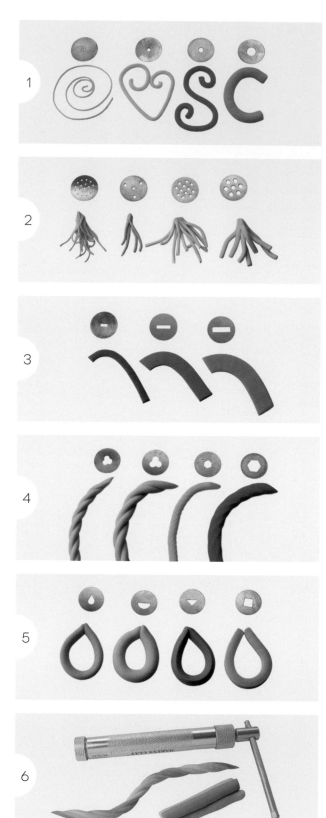

silicone border molds

Silicone border molds are designed to give a three-dimensional border. When working with these silicone molds, it is best to have a firm fondant. Knead additional powdered sugar into the rolled fondant to firm it up. Bead borders and rope borders are very common and can add an elegant or whimsical touch to any cake.

1 Roll a cylinder of softened fondant the length of the mold and a little larger in diameter than the mold size.

2 Open the mold and brush the inside with pearl dust. If matte finish is desired, dust the inside with cornstarch.

3 Open the mold and place it on the cylinder, which should remain on the work surface.

4 Open the mold slightly to ensure that fondant is fully filling the cavity—otherwise, the final border could be flat. Close the mold. Use a spatula to remove excess fondant from the top and side of the mold.

5 Open the mold using one hand and allow the border to fall out.

6 Attach the border to the cake with piping gel.

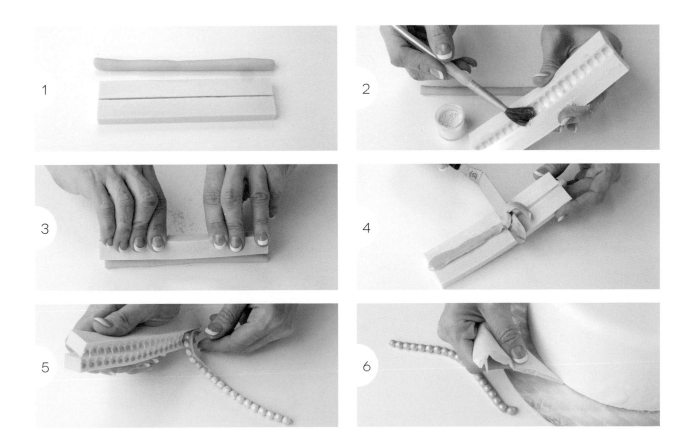

BEAD BORDER

1 The bead border shown here uses CK Products silicone mold for a full, three-dimensional border. Other bead molds may be easier to use, but the beads may have a flat back.

After releasing the string of beads, you may see a fine residue of fondant that resembles a string connecting the beads. If this is undesirable, allow the beads to form a crust and use a paring knife to trim off residue.

ROPE BORDER

2 A rope border can be used in a variety of themes. Add a festive touch to a western cake, the elegant look of draped fabric to a formal wedding cake, or a whimsical effect on a child's cake.

Once the rope is out of the mold, cut each end of the rope at an angle, following the lines from the twist of the rope. As you attach the rope to the cake, join the angled cut ends for a seamless look.

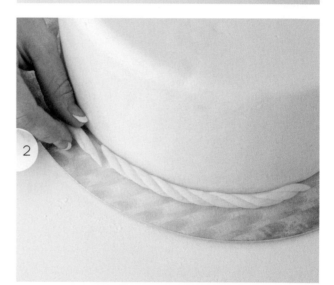

FINE POINTS OF BORDER MAKING

* When cleaning the silicone border molds, it may be difficult to remove colored dusting powders. Use only white pearl dust in the mold, or dust the piece with colored dusting powders after it has been molded.

* If fondant sticks to the silicone border molds, allow the fondant cylinder to set for a couple minutes before forming the mold around it.

* When forming the borders, the fondant should remain on the work surface. Do not hold the bead or rope maker open in one hand and try to feed the fondant into it with the other hand.

accents with silicone molds

Silicone molds give exquisite detail to rolled fondant or gum paste. Silicone easily picks up flecks of lint and dust. Wash the silicone mold with soap and water. Dry with a paper towel. Silicone mold making kits are available to create molds that are hard to find.

GENERAL SILICONE MOLDS

1 Knead and soften rolled fondant or gum paste. Form into a ball. Dust the ball with cornstarch.

2 Press ball into the mold, filling the entire cavity. Scrape off excess with a thin palette knife. Press against the edges of the cavity with fingers to ensure the edges are clean.

3 Hold the silicone mold with both hands and press in the center with thumbs to release the rolled fondant or gum paste.

LETTING GO

* If the silicone mold is deep or highly detailed, the rolled fondant or gum paste may be difficult to remove. If having difficulty removing the rolled fondant or gum paste, place the filled mold in the freezer for approximately 15 minutes to let it set more firmly.

* If the paste sticks to the mold, knead powdered sugar into the rolled fondant or gum paste to stiffen.

1

2

3

rolling and cutting gum paste and fondant

Many of the instructions in the following pages require rolling fondant or gum paste thin and cutting shapes. The thickness needed of the paste will vary depending on the project. Typically, the thinner the paste, the more delicate and professional the project will look. The #5 setting (0.4 mm) on a pasta machine or attachment is a nice thickness for most pieces that will be attached directly to the cake. A #4 setting (0.6 mm) on a pasta machine or attachment (slightly thicker than #5) is a nice thickness for pieces that will be standing up on a cupcake or cake.

Gum paste is ideal for more delicate-looking flowers and accents. Gum paste is more elastic and can be rolled more thinly than rolled fondant; 50/50 paste may also be used.

Follow these instructions for basic rolling and cutting instructions. It is important that the countertop is free of any debris or small particles.

1 Knead and soften gum paste or rolled fondant. Dust countertop surface with cornstarch. Roll paste thin using the 2 mm (or smallest size) perfection strips or use a pasta machine on a thin setting.

2 Rub the surface of a CelBoard or plastic placemat with a thin layer of solid vegetable shortening. Rub a thin layer of solid vegetable shortening on the cutting side of the cutter. The shortening should not be visible on the board or cutter. Place paste on CelBoard or plastic placemat.

3 Cut out shapes with desired cutter.

4 Pull away excess paste with a small palette knife.

5 Slide a long spatula with a thin blade under the cut piece. Lift the piece gently.

6 Attach the piece to the cake with piping gel or edible glue.

7 To add dimension to the cut piece place the cut piece on a former immediately after cutting. Allow to dry overnight.

COOKIE CUTTER CUTOUTS

Cookie cutters, fondant cutters, and gum paste cutters are available in dozens of shapes and designs. These cutouts will add a quick, simple decoration to any cake.

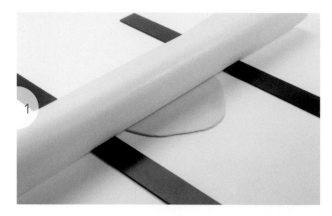

1 Knead and soften rolled fondant or gum paste. Roll paste to approximately ⅟₁₆" or 2 mm.

2 Cut shapes.

3 Attach the shapes to the cake with piping gel or edible glue immediately after they are cut so they will conform to the contour of the cake.

4 Layer the shapes for an eye-catching pattern. Create an inlay design with contrasting colors and smaller cutters. Cut small cutouts from the larger shape and replace with cutouts in a contrasting color.

SHARP CUTS

For the sharpest cut, be sure the cutter's edge is always clean and free of crusted rolled fondant or gum paste. Wipe with a damp cloth to remove crusted paste.

PLUNGER CUTTERS

Plunger cutters are gum paste cutters that cut flowers and other accents for cakes. Cut out simple flowers for quick decorations on any treat. The piece is cut, and then the plunger is pushed to release the cut piece. Many of the plungers have veining or details, which add extra charm to the cut piece. Gum paste or fondant can be used with plunger cutters. Roll gum paste and rolled fondant thin for delicate pieces.

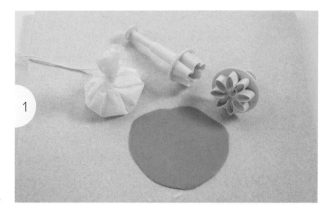

SIMPLE FLOWER PLUNGER CUTTERS

1 Knead and soften rolled fondant or gum paste. Dust work surface with cornstarch. Roll paste thin (#5 [0.4 mm] on a pasta machine). Dust the surface of a CelBoard or plastic placemat with cornstarch and place rolled paste on it.

2 Hold the plunger by the base and cut the shape. Lift the cutter. While the paste is still in the cutter, run thumb over the edges of the cutter to ensure a clean cut.

3 Press plunger to release flowers. Attach to cake with edible glue or cup petals following the subsequent directions.

4 Place small flowers on a piece of foam. Cup the petals with a ball tool. Place larger flowers in a flower former to cup the petals. Allow to dry. Attach flowers to cake with edible glue.

PLUNGER CUTTERS WITH VEINING AND DETAILING

1 Knead and soften rolled fondant or gum paste. Dust work surface with cornstarch. Roll paste thin (#4 [0.6 mm] on a pasta machine). Dust the surface of a CelBoard or plastic placemat with cornstarch and place rolled paste on it. Hold the plunger by the base and cut the shape.

2 Lift the cutter. While the gum paste is still in the cutter, run thumb over the edges of the cutter to ensure a clean cut.

3 Place cutter back onto work surface. Press the plunger to emboss the veins.

4 Lift and press plunger to release shape. Attach shapes to the cake with edible glue. If the cut shape sticks to the table, run a spatula with a very thin blade underneath the cut shape to lift it from work surface.

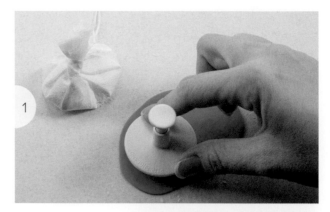

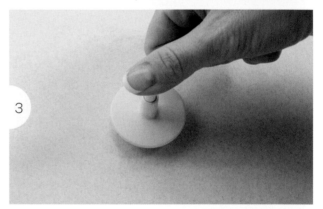

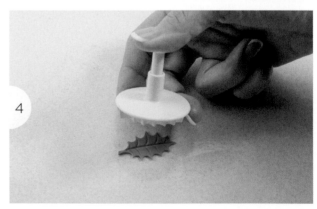

flower making basics

The subsequent chapters give instructions for creating popular flowers in gum paste. Gum paste allows the petals to be rolled very thin. This chapter covers basic techniques that can be used for most flowers. Step-by-step instructions show you how to create daisies, calla lilies, and roses. If you enjoy making these basic flowers, you will most certainly want to learn more. Dozens of other flower cutters are available, and there are many cake decorating books that deal exclusively with gum paste flowers.

Follow the basic flower-making instructions when creating most flowers. If possible, purchase a real flower to imitate the petals and colors as closely as possible. If the flower being created is not in season, look on the Internet for pictures to help emulate the flower. Egg whites can be used as glue for the flowers in this chapter if the gum paste pieces being glued are still soft. If the pieces are hard, edible glue should be used.

WRAPPING FLORIST WIRE

Some gum paste flowers require wires. Wires should be wrapped with floral tape to hide them. Floral tape—a reversible, narrow strip of crepe paper coated with wax—comes in white, green, and brown. Wrap the wire in white if it should not be seen, or if it will be inserted into a cake covered in white. Wrap the wire in green if the wire will be exposed and is meant to emulate a real flower stem. Use brown tape for branches and stems for flowers that blossom on trees, such as a flower from a dogwood tree.

1 Hold the wire in nondominant hand. Stretch the floral tape and twist to attach the tape to the wire. The stretching and warmth of your fingers releases and softens the wax, allowing the tape to stick to the wire and itself.

2 After the wire is covered, tear off the tape, leaving a little to spare. Stretch and wrap it back up on the wire.

3 The floral tape can be fed through a tape cutter to make it narrower. This is nice for dainty, small flowers so the wire doesn't get too bulky from the tape.

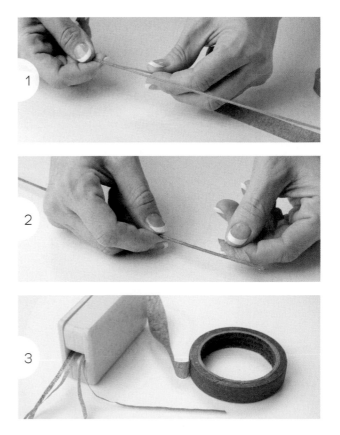

CUTTING AND SHAPING THE FLOWER PETALS

1 Knead and soften gum paste. Roll the paste very thin (a #5 on a pasta machine). The gum paste should be translucent. If it is not translucent, the petals will not be delicate. The thicker the paste, the easier it is to make the flowers, but the petals are not as lovely. Place the rolled gum paste on a CelBoard or a plastic placemat. Cut petals.

2 Place the petal on soft foam or a CelPad. Thin and shape petals by rubbing a ball tool along the petal's edges. The petal's edges should be very thin. Do not thin the center of the flowers.

3 Vein each petal by gently embossing with a veining tool. If the foam is too firm, the gum paste will tear when veins are added.

4 Some flowers, such as carnations, have ruffled petals. If the petals are to be frilled, the gum paste should be rolled with a #4 (0.6 mm) setting. If the petals are too thin, the edges will tear when ruffled. To frill the petals, place the petal along the edge of a CelPad. Roll a CelPin back and forth to thin and frill the edge. The amount of pressure used will determine the frilliness of the ruffle.

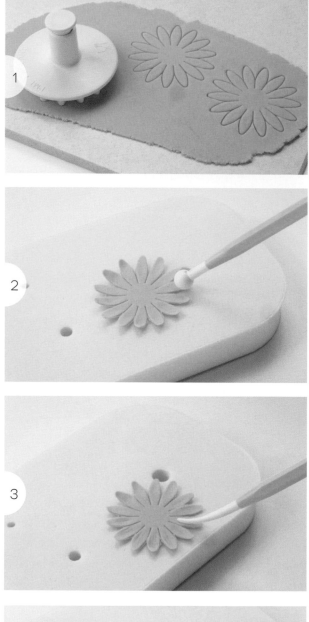

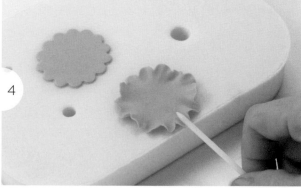

LEAVES

Several styles and sizes of leaf veiners are available. Many leaf cutters come with a veiner to match, or there are general leaf veiners.

1 Knead and soften gum paste. Dust work surface with cornstarch. Roll gum paste thin; leave one edge thick. With a leaf cutter, cut the gum paste, keeping the thick part at the bottom of the leaf.

2 Place the leaf on soft foam or a CelPad. Soften the edges of the leaf with a ball tool.

3 Hook the end of a wire. Dip the hooked end into egg whites. Press the hooked part of the wire into the thick part of the leaf.

4 Place cut leaf on a veiner lightly dusted with cornstarch. Firmly press to emboss.

HELPFUL TIPS

* Many flowers have coordinating veining mats. Press the mat into the cut flower after the petals have been softened and thinned.

* Place cut petals waiting to be thinned and veined under a CelFlap or sealed in a plastic bag in a single layer.

* If the petals stick to the CelBoard when cutting, lightly grease the board with a solid vegetable shortening and then wipe it off with a paper towel.

* Thoroughly knead and soften gum paste before rolling. If the gum paste is sticky, rub a small amount of grease on fingers. If the gum paste is dry and tough, soften it with a small amount of fresh egg whites.

LEAVES USING A CELBOARD

1 Hook the end of a wire. Dip the hooked end into egg white. Roll a small cylinder with green gum paste and form over the wire. Place the cylinder in one of the grooves in the CelBoard. Brush egg white on the top of the cylinder.

2 Knead and soften gum paste. Dust work surface with cornstarch. Roll gum paste thin (#5 [0.4 mm] on a pasta machine). Place the rolled gum paste on the CelBoard, covering the cylinder. Center the leaf cutter with the wire. Cut leaf.

3 Place the cut leaf on a CelPad. Soften the edges of the leaf with a ball tool. Place cut leaf on a veiner. Firmly press to emboss veins.

4 Double-sided veiners emboss veins on both sides of the leaf. Certain double-sided veiners will also give the leaf some shape.

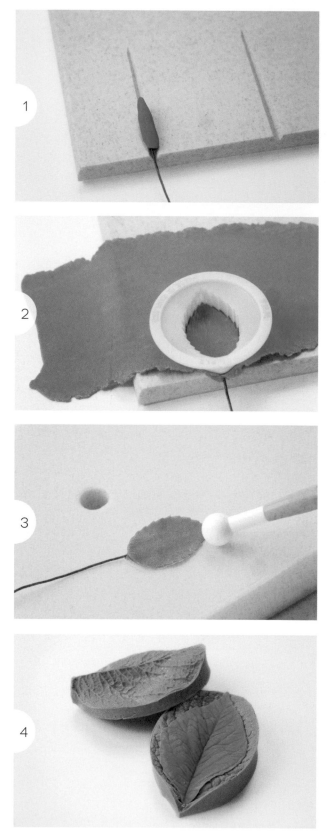

FLOWER SHADING

Shade the flower for a realistic effect. Start with gum paste in a pale shade of the flower or leaf to give a wide variety of color options. Brush the petals with dusting powders to shade.

1 Use a soft brush to give the flowers a subtle all-over dusting of color.

2 Use a flat, stiff brush to add an intense amount of color or to add color on the edges of the petals.

ADDING A SHINE TO FLOWERS AND LEAVES

3 Leaves, as well as flowers such as stepha-notis, look lovely and realistic with a subtle shine. Shine can be added with a steamer or with confectioner's glaze. An edible glaze is also available in an aerosol spray. This provides a natural shine. Because the glaze is sticky, the nozzle can get clogged, leaving a speckled glaze on the petals. Test the glaze on a sheet of parchment before spraying the petals to ensure a clean spray. Passing the flowers or leaves through the steam from a steamer will set the color and add a shiny, waxy appearance. Do not hold the flower still or the gum paste will begin to dissolve. Wave hand back and forth in front of the steamer for a few seconds or until the flower becomes shiny. Confectioner's glaze is a food-grade substance that adds a high shine. On its own, it is a thick, yellow substance. Using the glaze as is may add a yellow, thick layer. Thin the glaze with a neutral grain spirit. Stir equal parts alcohol and glaze. Dip the flowers into the mixture or brush the mixture onto each petal. The glaze may also be brushed onto the flower or leaf. If brushing, take care as the brush may leave brush strokes or streaks of color.

LOADING THE BRUSH

Tap the brush on the edge of the jar allowing excess dust to fall back into the jar. Too much dust on the brush may cause speckles of color or an uneven coat.

DRYING FLOWERS

1 Flower formers are available from several companies. Bowl-shaped flower formers are used to cup the flower. Flower former racks are used to hang flowers upside when drying.

Most flower formers have a hole in each cavity to allow the wire to extend. Rest the flower former on buckets to lift it off the work surface.

2 Make a simple hanging flower rack by placing a dowel on two equal size measuring cups.

ASSEMBLING FLOWERS

3 Wrap each flower stem with floral tape.

4 Arrange the flowers and secure with floral tape.

GERBERA DAISIES

Gerbera daisies are a popular cut flower available in a wide spectrum of vivid, lovely colors. Color the gum paste a soft pastel shade and accent with dusts to give a realistic appearance. The daisy can be a complicated flower to master, but the finished flower is outstanding. The cutters used for this project are daisy cutters sized 35 mm (calyx), 44 mm (center petals), and 85 mm. The circle cutter used is 1" (2.5 cm).

1 Knead and soften gum paste. Roll a ball about half the size of center of the daisy cutter and then flatten it. Roll a second ball half the size of the first. Bend a loop in the end of an 18-gauge wire and brush the loop with egg white.
  Press the small ball onto the loop. Pinch the ball to form a cone. Brush egg white on the top of the cone. Press the flattened ball on top of the cone. Pinch the flattened top with tweezers to give the center texture. Allow the daisy center to harden several hours or overnight.

2 Cut a small circle of softened gum paste, slightly larger than the daisy center. Brush egg white on the circle. Pierce the center of the circle with the wire, and bring the circle up around the hardened daisy center.

3 Use a pair of fine scissors and snip rows of tiny petals around the outside of the flat ball.

4 Roll softened gum paste thin, or a #5 (0.4 mm) on a pasta machine. Cut two flowers using a small daisy cutter. Place one flower under a CelFlap, or cover with plastic to prevent drying. Place the second flower on a CelPad. Soften the petals using a ball tool. Repeat for the other flower.

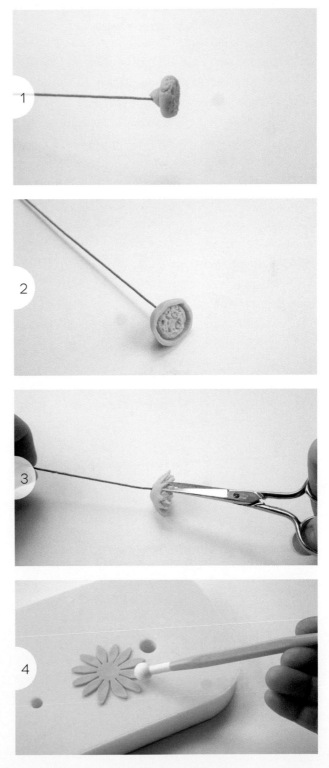

5 Brush center of one daisy with edible glue. Pierce center with the wire stem and slide up and around the flower center. Repeat with next daisy. Place in cone-shaped flower former.

6 Roll kneaded and softened gum paste thin (#5 [0.4 mm] on a pasta machine). Cut two large flowers with a cutter twice the size of the small cutter. Repeat step 4 with the first large daisy.

Add veins to each petal using the veining tool. Brush egg white on the center of one daisy. Pierce the center of the daisy with the wire stem, and bring the cut daisy up and around the center petals.

7 Repeat steps 4 and 6 with the second large daisy. Place the daisy in a cone flower former. Allow to dry at least 24 hours. When dry, dust the daisy with various shades of petal dusts.

8 To make the calyx, roll green gum paste thin. Cut a small daisy. Use a thin blade to make fine small cuts in each petal. Brush edible glue on the back of the calyx, pierce it with the wire stem, and bring it around the base of the daisy.

DAISY POINTERS

* The clear flower former shown has molds with holes to allow wires to poke through. If the holes are not big enough for the wire used, cut a larger hole with a pair of small pointed scissors. Prop the flower former to allow the wires to extend below.

* Softening and veining each petal requires a lot of time. Work quickly to keep the gum paste from tearing. If making gum paste from scratch, use less tylose if time is a concern.

ROSES

Roses are the most popular gum paste flower. The five-petal blossom cutter is used in these instructions. Single rose petal cutters are also available, but the five-petal cutter is easier for beginners.

ROSEBUD

1 Hook the end of an 18-gauge wire and brush the hook with egg white. Shape a ball of softened gum paste into a cone. Insert the wire hook into the wide end of the cone and taper the end of the cone around the wire. The cone should be nearly the length of one petal. Set aside for several hours or overnight.

Roll softened gum paste thin, or put through a pasta machine at #4 (0.6 mm). Cut one blossom shape using a five-petal blossom cutter and place it on a CelPad.

2 Soften and thin the edges of each petal with the ball tool. Then place the rounded end of the tool on each petal and press and roll slightly to cup the petals.

3 Place gum paste blossom onto a 3" (7.5 cm) square of thin foam for support. Brush egg white over the made-ahead cone. Push the wire stem through the center of the cut flower and foam.

4 The cut flower has five petals. Choose one petal as #1 and wrap around the cone.

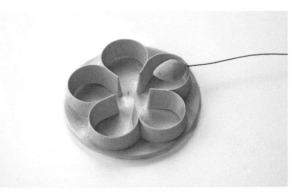

5 Counting counter-clockwise, brush egg white on the base of petal #3. Wrap around the cone. Brush egg white on the base of petal #5. Wrap around the cone.

6 Finally wrap petals #2 and #4 around the cone. Remove the finished rosebud from the foam. Add a calyx (see opposite), or continue with the following steps for a full rose.

ROSE

7 Make a rosebud following steps 1 through 6. Cut a second blossom and place the blossom on a Celpad. Soften and thin the edges of each petal with the ball tool. Cup petals #1 and #3. Turn cut blossom over and cup petals #2, #4, and #5. Turn the blossom back over and cup the middle so petals #1 and #3 face up. Set the blossom on a 3" (7.5 cm) piece of foam. Brush egg white on the base of the rosebud. Push the wire of the rosebud through the center of the newly made blossom and foam. Wrap petal #1 around the rosebud.

Brush egg white on the bottom half of petal #3. Wrap petal #3 around the rosebud. Brush egg white on the bottom half of petals #2, #4, and #5. Wrap around the rosebud.

8 Make a third blossom and wrap around the rose following step 7.

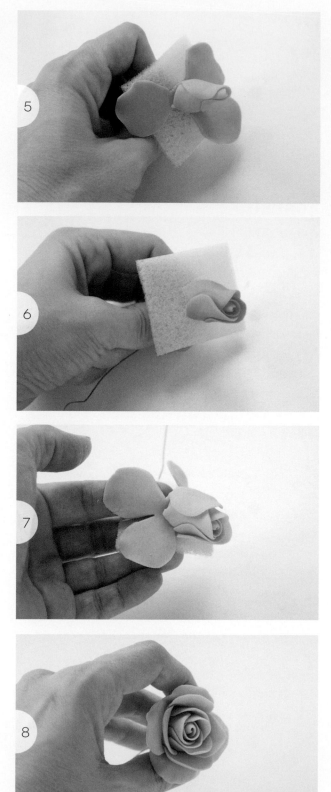

CALYX

1 Knead and soften gum paste. Roll gum paste thin, or a #4 on a pasta machine. Cut calyx. Thin the edges of the calyx. Cup the center with a ball tool.

2 Cut the sides of the calyx with fine scissors.

3 Brush the center of the calyx with egg white. Push the wire with the rosebud or rose into the center of the calyx. Press against the rose to secure. Roll a green gum paste ball and push up the wire. Form into a cone. Attach the cone to the bottom of the calyx, smoothing to appear as one piece.

4 Add leaves following directions on page 87. Dust the rose and leaves with various shades of dusting powders.

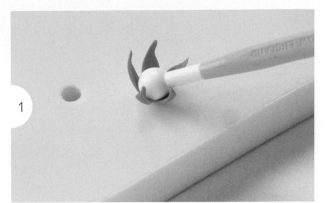

CALLA LILIES (ARUM LILIES)

The calla lily is one of the easiest gum paste flowers to create, but remember: Both the inside and outside are visible. Cutters are often labeled Arum cutters, though hearts may also be used.

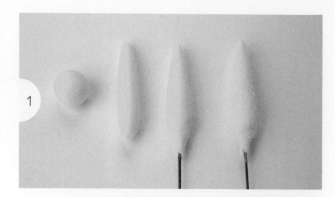

1 To make the spadix, roll a thin cone of softened yellow gum paste, about two-thirds the length of the cutter. Hook the end of an 18-gauge wire and brush it with edible glue. Form a yellow cone around the wire. Brush edible glue onto the cone and roll it in granulated sugar. Let dry.

Dust work surface with cornstarch. Roll softened white gum paste thin (#3 on a pasta machine). Dust a CelBoard or plastic placemat with cornstarch and place gum paste on it. Cut calla lily and then press both sides on a veiner. Use a veining tool down the center.

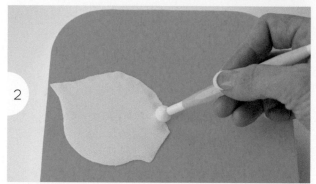

2 Place the lily petal on a CelPad. Soften the edges with a ball tool.

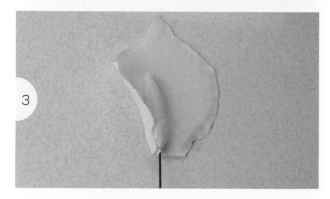

3 Brush a small amount of edible glue along the base of the cut flower. Place the spadix in the center then wrap one side of the calla lily around it. Next, tightly wrap the other side.

4 Shape the base of the flower and smooth around the wire. Slightly bend the edges and tip of the petal away from the stem then stand the flower in polystyrene foam to harden. When hardened, add three additional 18-gauge wires to the stem and wrap them together with floral tape.

Finally, brush chartreuse green petal dust on the base of the flower and apple green petal dust over it, blending upward. Brush apple green petal dust at the base of the spadix inside. Steam the flower to add a waxlike appearance.

BOWS

CURLY STREAMER BOW

A large, curly bow can be made with streamers cut the same length, or use many lengths and place the streamers across the cake for a festive design. Rolled fondant or 50/50 paste may be used.

1 Knead and soften gum paste. Dust work surface with cornstarch. Roll gum paste thin (#5 on a pasta machine), cut into ¼" × 10" (6 × 25 cm) strips, and wrap around wooden dowels.

2 After 5 to 10 minutes, remove streamers from dowels. If making a bow, cut streamers 3" (7.5 cm) long. If placing streamers loosely on the cake, cut them various lengths. Bend streamers while pliable for a natural curve.

3 When streamers are dry, pipe a ball of icing the same color as the cake. Arrange the streamers in a circle, pushing them into the icing to secure. Straight streamers should be placed first, then curved streamers.

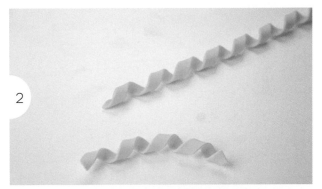

4 Add layers of streamers until the bow is full. Short or broken strips can add character.

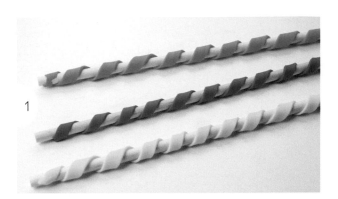

STREAMER TRICKS

* If the streamers crack or break when curved, allow less time on the dowels. If the streamers collapse when curved, allow more time.

* If several strips are cut at once, cover strips with a plastic wrap to keep from drying until strips are curled around the dowels.

GUM PASTE BOWS

The tie bow here is 3" (7.5 cm) wide and the loopy bow 7" (17.5 cm) wide; dimensions can be scaled up or down. Rolled fondant may be used for accent bows, but bows larger than 3" (7.5 cm) will be more stable when made of gum paste. A 50/50 blend of gum paste and fondant may be used.

TIE BOW

1 Knead and soften gum paste. Dust work surface with cornstarch. Roll gum paste thin (#5 [0.4 mm] on a pasta machine). Cover a CelBoard or plastic placemat with a thin layer of solid vegetable shortening and place the rolled gum paste on it.

Cut two 1" × 3" (2.5 × 7.5 cm) strips and brush the ends with edible glue. Fold the strips in half and pinch the ends together to form pleats.

2 For the bow streamers, cut two 1" × 3" (2.5 × 7.5 cm) strips of gum paste. Cut one end of each at an angle, and pinch the other end.

3 Put the streamers together and the folded loops on top. Cut a ½" × 1" (1.3 × 2.5 cm) strip for the knot. Pinch the ends.

4 Brush edible glue on the back of the knot and attach it to the bow, pressing the ends under the loops.

BOW TIPS

* If loops collapse, hold their shape with fiberfill. Remove it when the loop has dried.

* Bow cutters are available.

* Use a quilting tool for a stitched effect.

LOOPY BOW

1 Knead and soften gum paste. Dust work surface with cornstarch. Roll gum paste thin (#4 [0.6 mm] on a pasta machine). Rub the surface of a CelBoard or plastic placemat with a thin layer of solid vegetable shortening and place rolled gum paste on it.

Cut 1" × 6" (2.5 × 15 cm) strips of gum paste. A complete bow will require 18 strips. If all the strips are cut at once, place them in a single layer under plastic wrap to keep them from drying out. Brush the ends of the strips with edible glue. Fold the strips in half and stand the loop on its side to dry. Allow several hours to dry.

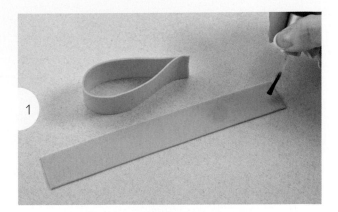

2 When the loops are dry, arrange them in a circle on the cake, leaving a 1" (2.5 cm) opening in the center. Fill the opening with a ball of royal icing the same color as the loops. Slightly push the arranged loops into the icing ball.

3 Add the next row of loops, inserting them into the icing.

4 Add a final layer of loops.

ENHANCING BOWS

The gum paste may be textured before cutting out the bow strips. Edible icing sheets can be used on top of the gum paste strips for a shimmer effect. Before you cut the strips, brush the back of the icing sheet with water and place the ribbon on the rolled gum paste.

RUFFLES AND FRILLS

Add a dainty touch to cakes with these ruffles. Ruffles can be made with a simple cut strip of 50/50 paste or with a frill cutter. The Garrett Frill Cutter was designed by cake decorator Elaine Garrett to create elegant ruffles with a natural curve. Straight frill cutters are available in several styles and ruffle widths.

FRILLS WITH THE GARRETT FRILL CUTTER

1 Mark the cake with the Smart Marker (page 35) to evenly space ruffle. For this design, every other hole was marked.

Dust work surface with cornstarch. Roll softened 50/50 paste thin (#4 [0.6 mm] on a pasta machine). Rub the surface of a CelBoard or plastic placemat with a thin layer of solid vegetable shortening and place rolled paste on it. Cut with the Garrett Frill Cutter and remove the center circle.

2 Cut the ring open with a paring knife. Place the strip close to the edge on a foam pad. Roll a CelPin back and forth to thin and frill the edge. The amount of pressure used will determine the frilliness.

3 Pipe dots of piping gel on top of the marked indents in the cake and attach the ruffle swag to them. Add a couple of dots of piping gel in the center behind the swag to secure.

4 Additional swags may be added. Pipe a line of piping gel just above the top edge of the first ruffle. Attach the second ruffle just above the first ruffle, following the curve. Pipe a dainty border to give the ruffle a finished edge.

STRAIGHT FRILL CUTTERS

1 Dust work surface with cornstarch. Roll softened 50/50 paste thin (#4 [0.6 mm] on a pasta machine). Rub the surface of a CelBoard or plastic placemat with a thin layer of solid vegetable shortening and place rolled paste on it. Cut the paste using a straight frill cutter.

2 Place the strip close to the edge on the soft side of a foam pad. Roll a CelPin back and forth to thin and frill the edge. The amount of pressure used will determine the frilliness of the ruffle.

3 Pipe small dots of piping gel on the back of the ruffle. Do not put the close to the top edge or the piping gel may seep out. Attach the ruffle to the top edge of the cake. To add additional ruffles, trim the top edge of the new ruffle approximately ¼" (6 mm).

4 Place a small amount of piping gel on the back of the new ruffle and attach. Any additional ruffles should be trimmed a bit more than the previous ruffle. Pipe a dainty border to finish the edge.

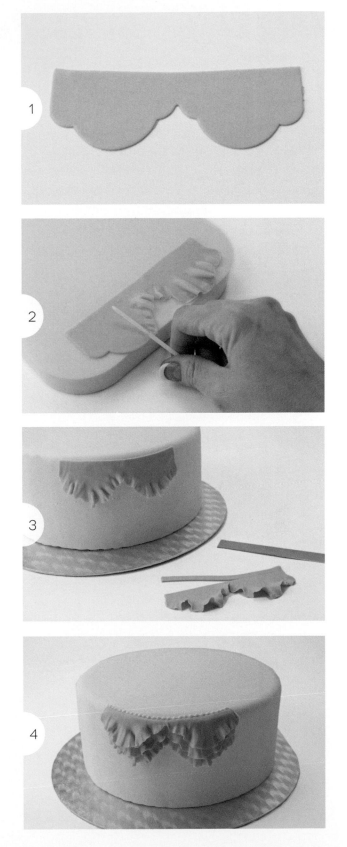

basic shapes for hand modeling

The next few sections cover hand modeling, or hand molding, animals and people. Gum paste is best for stability when hand modeling. Here you'll learn five basic shapes that can be hand modeled. Each animal or person will use some of these shapes. Before beginning to shape, knead and soften the gum paste until smooth. It is very important that the work surface and hands are clean as gum paste picks up tiny specks of dust.

BALL

1 All shapes start with a ball. Roll paste gently in your palms until an even, ball shape is formed.

EGG

2 Roll a smooth ball. Form a V shape with your hands. Roll the ball back and forth in a sliding motion until one edge is slightly tapered.

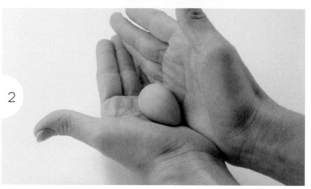

TEARDROP

3 The teardrop is made like the egg. Form a V shape with your hands and roll the ball back and forth in a sliding motion until one edge is slightly tapered. The longer you roll the egg back and forth, the more tapered the egg becomes.

CYLINDER

4 Roll a smooth ball. Place the ball on the work surface and roll using your palms. It is important to use uniform pressure so that the cylinder is even throughout. Using fingertips to roll will give an uneven cylinder.

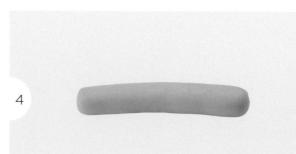

CURVY CYLINDER

5 Adding curves is important when forming arms and legs. Without curves, arms and legs look like spaghetti. Place the cylinder on your work surface and roll using your index finger to create curves.

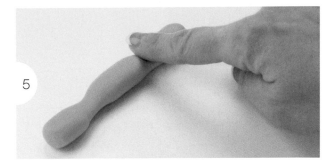

6 You can also add curves by picking up the cylinder and rolling it between your index finger and thumb. Be careful, if the gum paste is too soft, the cylinder will stretch.

MODELING TOOLS

7 A Polyblade is a thin, flexible blade that will cut easily through gum paste. Slide the blade back and forth and gently cut through the gum paste. Do not cut with a quick, straight motion down, or the gum paste may have a flattened edge.

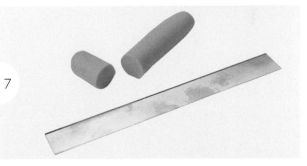

8 A variety of ball tools are useful for embossing.

9 Use either end of a round tip for embossing mouths, depending on the size you want.

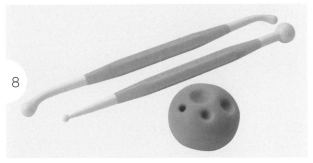

WRINKLE FREE

If you notice wrinkles when shaping, press the gum paste firmly in your palms, flattening to smooth the paste. When flattened and smoothed, roll into a ball. If there are still wrinkles, add a bit of shortening to your palms before kneading.

HAND-MODELING ANIMALS

Hand-molded, or hand-modeled, animals are adorable on cakes and cupcakes. These instructions are for basic bodies for standing and sitting animals. Changing the face, ears, and tail will distinguish the type of animal. Gum paste is best suited for this, the amount of which for each animal part is given in grams. Most digital scales convert ounces to grams easily.

STANDING ANIMALS

Standing animals are among the easiest figures to create. Even a young child can hand-mold these simple characters.

1 Knead and soften gum paste. Form a teardrop for the body (26 g).

2 Bend the teardrop for a neck so it resembles a paisley shape.

3 Roll a cylinder (13 g) and cut it into four equal parts. Stand the four parts to create legs and brush the tops of the legs with edible glue.

4 Place the body on the legs. Insert a toothpick or dried spaghetti through the neck. The body, neck, and legs can be stretched for long, thin animals, such as a giraffe.

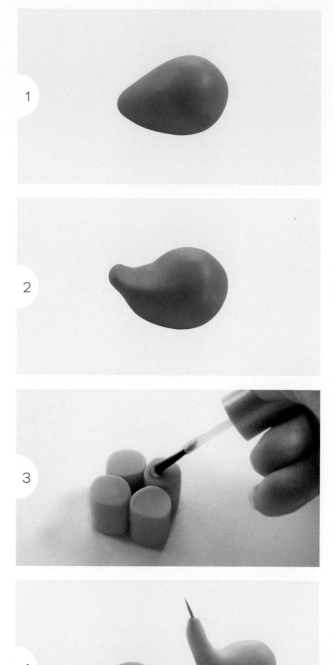

SITTING ANIMALS

Easy to shape and adorable, these sitting characters resemble stuffed animals. The bodies, arms, and legs can be stretched for animals with long arms, such as a monkey, or kept short for chubby animals, such as a fat teddy bear.

1 Form a teardrop for the body (25 g). Stand the cone upright and place a toothpick through the teardrop.

2 Roll two cylinders for the legs (7 g each). Add curves and dimension to form thighs, ankles, and feet.

3 Roll two more cylinders for the arms (3 g each). Add curves and dimension to form shoulders, wrists, and hands.

4 Attach the legs and then the arms to the body with edible glue.

NO SLOUCHING

* If the animals sag, the gum paste is too soft. Knead a small amount of tylose into the gum paste to stiffen.

* A toothpick is used to give the animal stability while molding. A toothpick can be a choking hazard. Any time a toothpick is used, make sure those serving the cake are aware of them. Advise them to set aside the characters before serving the cake. Never use a cut or partial toothpick. Dried spaghetti or other thin pastas can be used as an alternative to a toothpick, but dried pasta is more delicate and may break while molding the character.

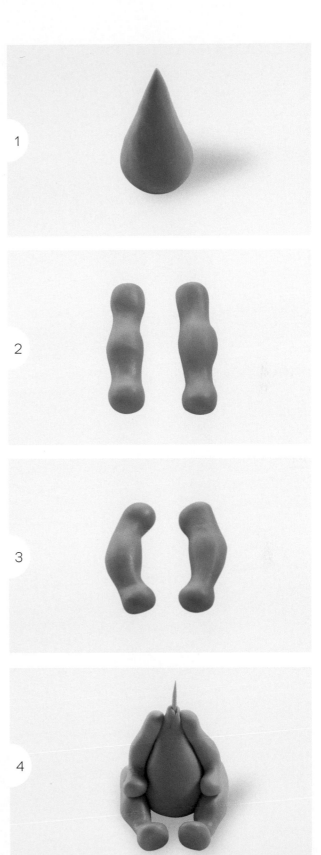

ROUND ANIMAL FACES

After the standing or sitting body is formed, the animal face is next. The instructions for the indented eyes are made using a ball tool and black fondant. See page 114 for alternatives when making eyes.

1 Roll a ball for the head (13–14 g). Place the ball in a flower former to keep the round shape while adding the details. In the center of the ball, make two indentations for the eyes using a ball tool.

2 With a paring knife or a thin, small spatula, make a V on its side in the eye indentations.

3 Roll a small ball for the muzzle and then flatten it into an oval. Cut through the center of the oval.

4 Attach the muzzle to the face with edible glue.

5 Roll two small balls for the eyes. Add a dot of edible glue in the eye indentation. Insert eyes. Roll a small ball for the nose. Flatten the ball and shape into a triangle for the nose. Attach to the muzzle with edible glue.

6 Brush the toothpick on the animal body with a small amount of edible glue. Attach the face to the body. Attach the ears with edible glue (instruction for different types of ears following). Most animals' ears will be placed at 10:00 and 2:00. Monkeys' ears look better placed centered on the head (or 9:00 and 3:00).

OVAL ANIMAL FACES

Animals with long faces such as horses, giraffes, zebras, and sheep start with an egg shape.

7 Form an egg shape.

8 Place the egg shape in a flower former. Use your pinky to indent for the nose and brow. Complete the oval animal head using steps 1 through 6 above.

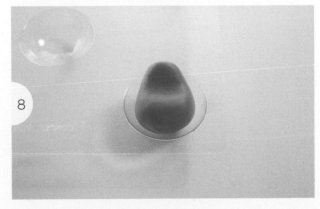

ANIMAL EARS

The shape and size of animal ears will vary according to the animal.

1 **Round Ears:** Form two balls the same size. Cup the ball with a ball tool to form the lobe.

2 Cut the bottom quarter so the ear will conform to the shape of the head.

3 **Pointed Ears:** Form two balls the same size. Cup the ball with a cone tool to form the lobe.

4 Stretch the ears over the cone and cut the bottom quarter so the ear will conform to the shape of the head.

5 **Floppy Ears:** Form two balls and cup the ball with a rounded tool or the end of a paint brush. Stretch the ears over the tool.

6 Pinch the ends together to form a teardrop and cut the bottom quarter so the ear will conform to the shape of the head.

ANIMAL TAILS

Use these tails for sitting or standing animals. Long tails and curly tails should be made several hours ahead of time to allow to dry before attaching to the body or they will lose their shape or break. Short tails may be added at any time to the body.

1 **Long Tails:** Roll a thin cylinder and curve to the desired shape. Allow to dry for several hours before attaching to the body with edible glue.

2 **Fluffy Tails:** Roll a ball and add texture with a star tip, such as tip #16. Attach to the body with edible glue.

3 **Curly Tails:** Roll a very thin cone and wrap around a toothpick. Allow to dry for several hours. Attach to the body with edible glue.

4 **Stubby Tails:** Form a cone and curve to form a paisley shape. Attach to the body with edible glue.

ADDING CONTRASTING PATTERNS TO THE ANIMALS

5 Paint the animal with concentrated food color. Allow the food color to dry completely before touching the animal.

6 Spots can also be made with gum paste rolled thin and formed in various shapes and sizes.

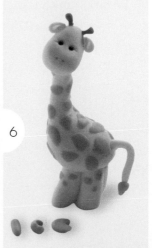

HAND-MODELING PEOPLE

This section covers instructions for creating standing and sitting people. The body, face, hands, and feet should be made the first day. On the second day add details to the eyes and sculpt the hair. The amount of gum paste needed for the projects is listed in grams, which are more accurate than ounces. Most digital scales have ounce-to-gram conversion capabilities.

SITTING PEOPLE

1 Form a ball (10 g) for the waist and two cylinders (11 g each) for the legs. Flatten the waist and add curves in the cylinders to form the knees and ankles. Cut the upper corner of the leg at an angle and attach to the waist with edible glue. Use a paring knife to cut wrinkles in the bend of the back of the knees.

2 Form two cones (6 g each) for the arms and one cone (19 g) for the chest.

3 Attach the chest to the waist with edible glue. Add curves to the arms to form the wrists and elbows, cutting wrinkles in the bend of the elbow with a paring knife. Form two egg shapes for the shoes (3 g each) and add dimension by gently pressing.

4 Attach the shoes and arms with edible glue. Press a toothpick down through the chest.

Form the head following instructions on page 112. Insert the head through the toothpick. Make hands according to directions on page 115. Each hand is 1 g. Allow the head to harden several hours or overnight. Finish the piece by adding hair.

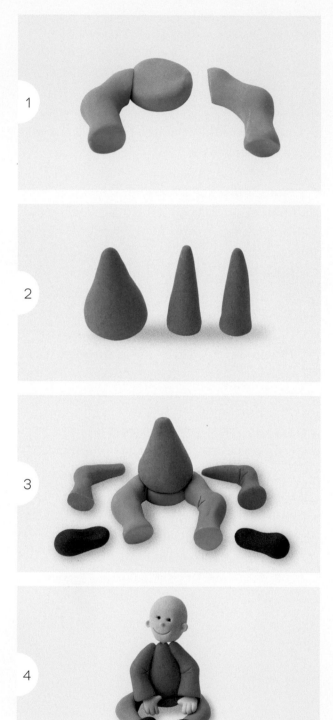

STANDING PEOPLE

1 Form two balls for the shoes (3 g each). Using the same color, form a ball (10 g) for the waist and two cones (11 g each) for the legs.

2 Flatten the waist. Roll the shoe balls into an oval, adding dimension by gently pressing. Add curves to the legs to form the knees and ankles. Gently insert a wooden skewer through the legs, being careful not to distort any details.

3 Place the shoes on polystyrene foam. Add a touch of edible glue to the back of the shoe. Insert the skewers with the leg attached through the shoes and polystyrene foam. Brush edible glue on the tops of the legs. Push the waist through skewer, resting on the top of the legs. Form one cone (19 g) for the chest and two cones (6 g each) for the arms.

4 Brush edible glue on top of the waist and insert the chest cone. Add curves to the arms to form the wrists and elbows. Use a paring knife to cut wrinkles in the bend of the elbow then attach the arms with edible glue.

Add a bit of edible glue to the neck area. Gently press a toothpick through the chest. Form the head following instructions on page 112. Insert head through the toothpick. Make hands according to directions on page 115. Each hand is 1 g. Allow the head to harden several hours or overnight. Finish the piece by adding hair.

HAND-MOLDING FACES

1 Form an egg shape (13 g) and place in a flower former. Make an indentation in the center of the face to form the forehead.

2 Pinch the chin to define the jaw.

3 Add the mouth using a round cake decorating tip, such as tip #1A.

Choose a type of eyes using the techniques shown on page 114. If making hollow eyes, form two indentations using the ball tool. Otherwise, do not hollow the eyes.

Roll a ball for the nose and attach with edible glue. Form two small balls for the ears and add dimension with a ball tool. Attach to the face. Finish the eyes following instructions on page 114.

FACIAL FEATURE PLACEMENT

Follow these guidelines for general face placement when hand-molding faces. Divide the face into three equal sections from the top of the forehead to the bottom of the chin. The halfway mark (dotted line) should be in the center of the middle third. The eyebrow line rests under the top third. The eyes are just above the center line. The nose line is just above the bottom third. The ears are centered. Vary the size and placement of facial features to give each face a distinct look.

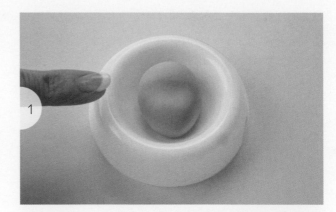

MAKING FACES FROM A MOLD

1 Form a teardrop. Place the tip of the teardrop into the nose cavity.

2 Press the fondant to form the head, keeping a nice, round shape to the back of the head.

3 Remove the face from the mold. Smooth any showing seam and place in a flower former.

4 Make two pin holes in the nostrils. Add shape to the mouth using a round cake decorating tip, such as tip #12. Add indentations for the eyes using a ball tool. Finish the eyes following the instructions opposite.

5 Form two small balls for the ears. Use a ball tool to add dimension. Attach to the face.

MAKING THE EYES

1 Roll two white balls the same size. Paint a dot of edible glue in the eye indentation. Insert the balls level with the indentation. If the balls are too small, the eyes will look sunken; too large and they will look bug-eyed.

2 Allow the white balls to dry several hours. Paint a colored iris and a black pupil with food color and a fine brush or use a food marker with a fine tip. Then outline the eye and add eyelashes and eyebrows. Allow the eye to completely dry. Add a dot in the black pupil with white food color.

3 Eyes can also be made with two tiny, equal-sized balls of black gum paste. Make indentations with a tiny ball tool when forming the face. Use a paring knife to cut a sideways V in each eye. Paint a dot of edible glue in the eye indentation. Insert the rolled balls. These eyes can make the face look scary if the rolled black balls are too large. The eyes should be very tiny.

4 The eyes may also be painted. Leave the face smooth without any eye indentations. Use white food color and paint the white of the eye. Let it dry completely. Paint a colored iris and a black pupil with food color and a fine brush or a food marker with a fine tip. Then outline the eye.

MATCHING EYES

When making eyes, roll one ball and then roll the other. Do not roll a ball, put it in the indentation, and then roll the second ball. It is very difficult to duplicate the same size of eyes without seeing the balls side by side.

HANDS AND FEET

Hands and feet look difficult to master, but are really quite easy to achieve. The fingers and toes are thin and may dry out, wrinkle, or fall off while shaping if not worked quickly. The hands have four fingers and the feet have four toes. This gives the figures a cartoon feel. If a more realistic figure is desired, cut five fingers and toes. The amount of gum paste needed is for the figures for the sitting and standing people. One gram of gum paste is needed for the hands. If an arm is to be made (shown), 4 g of gum paste is needed. If simple egg-shape shoes are to be made or just the feet are to be made, 3 g of gum paste is required for each shoe. If a leg is to be made, 6 g will be required.

Hands

1 Knead and soften 4 g of gum paste. Form a cylinder for the arm and then roll it between your thumb and index finger to form the hand and create a curve for the wrist.

2 Flatten the hand. With a blade, cut the hand in a mitt shape.

3 Use the blade to cut three additional fingers.

4 Separate the fingers and gently roll each finger between your thumb and index finger to smooth sharp edges and lengthen the thumb.

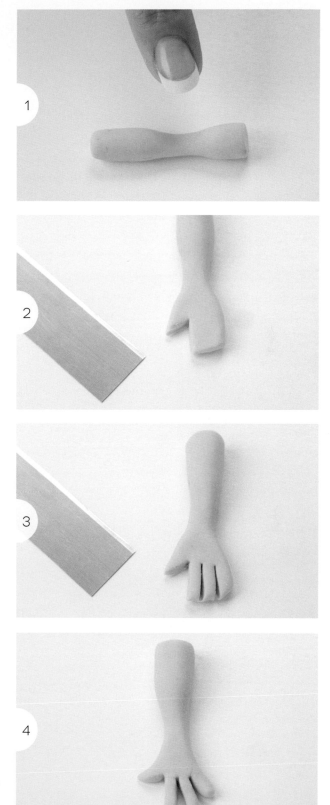

Feet

1 Knead and soften 6 g of gum paste. Form a cylinder for the leg. Bend the cylinder to the form a foot.

2 Form a curve at the ankle by rolling the cylinder between two fingers.

3 Pull out the heel to make the heel protrude. Stand the foot upright and press gently to flatten the bottom of the foot.

4 Pinch the foot in the middle to add an arch. Flatten the foot so it slopes downhill. Use a blade to cut three lines for the toes and then round and smooth the toes with your fingers.

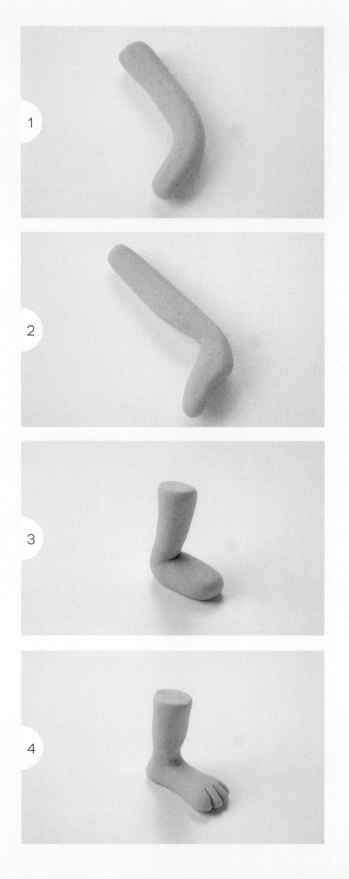

HAIR

Allow the head to dry at least 24 hours before adding hair. Short hair can be added at any time after the head has hardened. After texturing long hair, immediately put the head on the body, so that the hair will form around the shoulders.

Straight and Curly Hair

1 Roll a ball and flatten to a thin, misshapen oval to fit the length of hair desired. One end should be thinner than the other. Brush edible glue on the head where the hair will be placed and attach hair, with the thin end on the forehead.

2 **Straight Hair:** Use a paring knife to engrave lines (do not cut too deeply). Cut through the edges of the bottom of the hair to separate the strands.

3 **Curly Hair:** Use a paring knife to create a part. Use a toothpick and carve C's to create a curly texture over the entire length of hair.

Fine Hair Strands

4 Roll kneaded and softened gum paste into a cylinder. Place in a clay extruder fitted with fine holes. Brush edible glue on the head where the hair will be placed and attach hair. Continue adding texture over the entire length of hair.

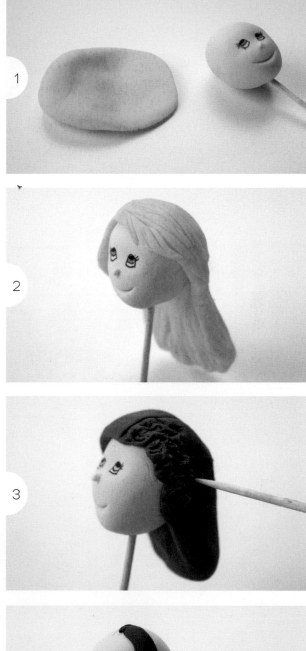

MISCELLANEOUS TECHNIQUES

This section covers additional methods to enhance decorating. Learn how to add sparkle and shine to treats. See how easy it is to create cakes with edible pictures. This section also covers beginning basics on product usage and useful tools, including the airbrush. Find out how to add patterns and paint on fondant.

stencils

Stencils are a great way to add details quickly. It is important the cake's surface is as smooth and flat as possible before using a stencil. Rolled fondant-covered cakes give the best effect, but other icings may be used. Let the rolled fondant-covered cake form a firm crust for several hours. Otherwise, indents may show from pressing on the stencil. Buttercream may also be used. Allow the buttercream several hours to crust. Use buttercream icing instead of royal icing when icing over the stencil.

ADDING A PATTERN WITH ICING

1 Place stencil on the cake. Mix royal icing according to directions. Thin the royal icing with water so that the royal icing has a soft peak. Put a small scoop of royal icing on one end of the stencil.

2 Spread the royal icing along the stencil using a small scraper.

3 Peel back the stencil.

STENCIL SHIFTING

To prevent the stencil from moving, rub a small amount of solid vegetable shortening on the back of the stencil. Use very little shortening, as the grease may spot the rolled fondant.

adding shimmer and sparkle to cakes

Add a touch of sparkle to cakes with fun sprinkles or dusts. Check each product to be sure it is suitable for consumption. Non-toxic products not FDA approved may be used for decorations but should be removed before serving.

EDIBLE GLITTER AND COARSE SUGARS

1 The fine flakes of edible glitter add a slight shimmer—a little bit will go a long way. It is best used when sprinkled all over the cake as it is difficult to cover small areas. Sanding sugar is coarser than granulated cane sugar. Coarse sugar is even coarser. The coarser the grain, the more sparkle.

For a buttercream iced cake, sprinkle the glitter or coarse sugar onto the cake before the buttercream crusts. For a fondant-covered cake, or a buttercream crusted cake, brush a thin layer of piping gel on the area to be covered, then sprinkle the glitter or coarse sugar on the piping gel.

DUSTING POWDERS

Dusting powders are available in a variety of finishes and give an all-over metallic finish. Luster dust comes in dozens of colors. Pearl dusts have a pearlized white finish. Lighten luster dust colors with super pearl, a basic white shimmer that will add a sheen to any color. Mix super pearl dust with matte colors (petal dusts) to give the color a shimmer, although the color may lighten a bit. Sparkle dusts have a coarser grain, which makes the sparkle a little more brilliant. Ultra white sparkle is especially pretty on flowers for a shimmery, dewy effect. Dusting powders can be brushed on dry, or the powder can be mixed with grain alcohol.

Brushing on Dry Dust

2 Use parchment paper to cover areas where dust is not wanted. Buttercream iced cakes may end up looking streaked if brushed with dusting powders. Consider a metallic edible spray instead. Dusting powders may be brushed onto buttercream piped flowers or accents. Freeze the accents and then bring one out at a time, quickly brushing on the dusting powder.

Painting on Dry Dust

3 Add just a few drops of grain alcohol to the dust so the dust is no longer a powder. Brush the paint onto any media that is firm, such as gum paste, rolled fondant, or dried royal icing accents.

edible frosting sheets

Edible frosting sheets are pictures printed on edible paper with food color. Edible sheets come in top designs, side designs, full sheets designs, and ribbons. Printers with edible ink cartridges can be purchased to print edible pictures from home, but they can be costly. Sometimes local cake and candy supply stores print pictures.

EDIBLE PRE-PRINTED DESIGNS

1 These edible sheets are manufactured for quick application for the top of the cake. Edible pre-printed designs are available in many themes and most popular licensed characters.

EDIBLE FROSTING STRIPS AND RIBBONS

2 Edible frosting strips add a vibrant band around a cake. Edible frosting ribbon sheets replace fabric ribbons, which look lovely around a cake, but may soak up grease and leave unattractive grease spots.

PRINTED SHEETS

3 Use these vibrant edible sheets for an all-over print on cakes, or decorate cookies and cupcakes. Cut out accents for a patterned decoration.

GENERAL INSTRUCTIONS FOR BUTTERCREAM

Bake and ice cake. With the image facing up, slide the edible frosting sheet over the edge of a countertop to release the image. Remove image from paper backing and place edible frosting sheet on the cake.

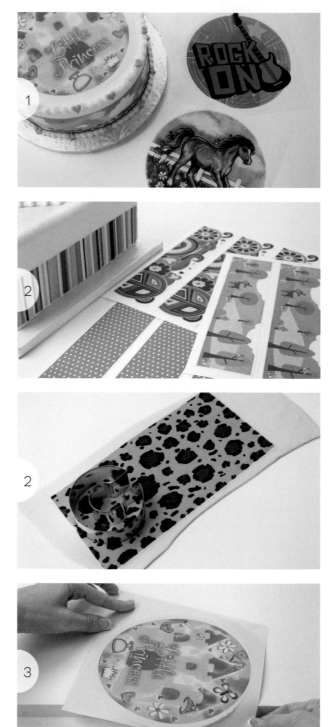

painting and coloring on fondant

White fondant is a blank canvas to paint details with food color or color with markers. Draw artwork, print clip art, or use coloring pages. Allow the fondant to crust before painting, or brushes and markers will leave indentations.

PAINTING WITH FOOD COLORS

1 Outline the back of the image with a nontoxic pencil. A lightbox is useful to see the outline.

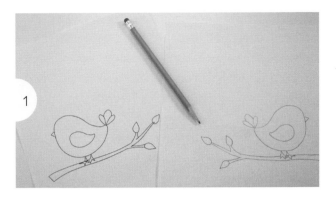

2 Allow fondant-covered cake to form a crust. Hold the nontoxic pencil almost parallel to the top of the cake. Rub over the front side of the image with the pencil to transfer design onto fondant. Lift the paper. The image will be faint, but strong enough to use as a guide for coloring.

3 Thin food color with water. Paint fondant-covered cake, leaving a little bit of space between each color to keep colors from bleeding.

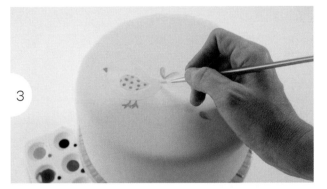

4 Outline the design with a black food color pen.

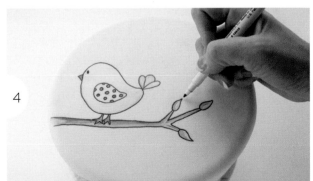

PAINTING TIPS

* Test the color of the food color paint on a sheet of white paper before painting directly on the cake to ensure the color is as desired.

* Be careful not to rest wrist or hand on the cake while painting.

* Use just enough color on the brush so the bristles are damp. Too much water will cause the sugar in the rolled fondant to dissolve.

airbrushing

Airbrush equipment has become increasing popular. Today the airbrush is used in cake decorating for shading, detailing a cake, stenciling onto a cake, and efficiently adding color all over the cake. An airbrush may be used on most types of icings. Buttercream and rolled fondant are among the most common types of icings to use as a background "canvas" for the airbrush color. The oils in ganache icings may cause the water-based airbrush color to puddle, so these types of icings are not well-suited for airbrushing.

Airbrushes used in cake decorating are typically single-action or dual-action. On single-action airbrushes, the air and the food color are released at the same time when the trigger is pulled. In dual-action airbrushes, the air is controlled separately by the compressor and the amount of airbrush color released is controlled by the pull of the trigger. Dual-action may take extra practice to master compared to a single-action airbrush. The instructions in this chapter are using Kopykake brand, single-action airbrush. The needles on all types of airbrushes are very fragile. Needles can be bent or damaged, in which case the airbrush will not function properly. Only use airbrush food color in the airbrush gun. Other colors may clog and ruin the airbrush. Do not thin gel or paste colors with water. Do not add water to powdered color to make a liquid color.

An air source is required for an airbrush. A compressor is the most common source of air in cake decorating. Purchase a compatible compressor based on the amount of pressure (PSI) needed for the airbrush. Be sure the air compressor has enough pressure to secure an even flow of color.

GENERAL INSTRUCTIONS

1 Fill the airbrush color cup approximately half full.

2 Use parchment paper to cover any area of the cake where airbrush color should not be applied. Hold the airbrush at a 45° angle. Pull the trigger to control the air flow. Hold the airbrush 6" to 8" (15 × 20 cm) from the cake to cover a wide area. Do not quickly move the hand back and forth or the color will be blotchy. Pull the trigger to begin spraying the cake with color. Do not hold the airbrush stationary, or puddles of food color will begin to form. Spray the cake with long, slow, and steady strokes.

3 If a second color is desired, rinse the airbrush before adding an additional color. Follow the manufacturer's directions for rinsing the airbrush.

4 Hold the airbrush close for fine details or shading. The trigger is barely pulled back to release a very fine stream of color. Food color sprays give an all-over airbrush effect without the expense of an airbrush. Fine details cannot be obtained using the food color sprays. Use the airbrush to efficiently color buttercream, royal icing, rolled fondant, or gum paste flowers.

resources

The supplies used in this book may be found at your local cake and candy supply store or from Country Kitchen SweetArt, 4621 Speedway Drive, Fort Wayne, Indiana 46825, 260-482-4835, www.shopcountrykitchen.com.

about the author

 Autumn Carpenter's passion for decorating started at a young age. As a child, Autumn would spend time at the home of her grandmother, Hall of Fame sugar artist Mildred Brand. Her mother, Vi Whittington, became the owner of a retail cake and candy supply shop. Her grandmother provided many recipes, while her mother instilled a work ethic, a passion for the art, and served as the best teacher and mentor that Autumn has ever had.

Autumn has served as a judge in cake decorating competitions. She is a Hall of Fame sugar artist and a member, teacher, and demonstrator at the International Cake Exploration Society (ICES) for nearly 20 years.

Autumn is co-owner of Country Kitchen SweetArt, a retail cake and candy supply store owned and operated within Autumn's family for over 45 years. Visit the store in person or online at www.shopcountrykitchen.com.

Autumn has developed her own line of cake decorating tools and equipment. Her products can be found online as well as in many cake and candy supply stores. Autumn's other websites include www.autumncarpenter.com and www.cookiedecorating.com.

acknowledgments

This book is dedicated to my children: Isaac, Austin, Sydney, and Simon who are always a source of inspiration. This book is also dedicated to my mom, Vi Whittington, who instilled my love of cake decorating at a very young age. My mom also had an essential role in the completion of this book, serving as a mentor, dishwasher, housekeeper, chauffeur, and babysitter.

I would also like to thank my husband, and business partner, Bruce Carpenter, who provides tremendous support in all my ventures.

index